D0122598

THE NEW
ADVANTAGE

THE NEW ADVANTAGE

How Women in Leadership Can Create Win-Wins for Their Companies and Themselves

HOWARD J. MORGAN AND JOELLE K. JAY

Foreword by Marshall Goldsmith,
New York Times *best-selling author*

 PRAEGER™

An Imprint of ABC-CLIO, LLC
Santa Barbara, California • Denver, Colorado

Library of Congress Cataloging-in-Publication Data

Names: Morgan, Howard J., author. | Jay, Joelle K. (Joelle Kristin), 1970- author.
Title: The new advantage : how women in leadership can create win-wins for their companies and themselves / Howard J. Morgan, Joelle K. Jay ; foreword by Marshall Goldsmith.
Description: 1 Edition. | Santa Barbara, California : Praeger, 2016.
Identifiers: LCCN 2015047035 | ISBN 9781440844591 (hardback) | ISBN 9781440844607 (ebook)
Subjects: LCSH: Leadership in women. | Success in business. | BISAC: BUSINESS & ECONOMICS / Leadership.
Classification: LCC HQ1233 .M637 2016 | DDC 303.3/4082—dc23
LC record available at http://lccn.loc.gov/2015047035

ISBN: 978-1-4408-4459-1
EISBN: 978-1-4408-4460-7

20 19 18 17 16   1 2 3 4 5

This book is also available on the World Wide Web as an eBook.
Visit www.abc-clio.com for details.

Praeger
An Imprint of ABC-CLIO, LLC

ABC-CLIO, LLC
130 Cremona Drive, P.O. Box 1911
Santa Barbara, California 93116-1911

This book is printed on acid-free paper ∞

Manufactured in the United States of America

This book is dedicated to our mothers, Heidi Morgan and Evelyn Grupe. They have lived in a different time and have seen the points in history that have started the new advantage for women. Both of us, and they, hope that they will see even more change during their lives.

Contents

Foreword by Marshall Goldsmith ix

He Said, She Said xiii

Introduction: The New Advantage xvii

1 The Networking Advantage
   (How do you connect to influencers?) 1

2 The Balance Advantage
   (How do you succeed without the stress?) 17

3 The Sponsorship Advantage
   (How do you acquire champions?) 37

4 The Executive Presence Advantage
   (How do you know you're perceived as a leader?) 55

5 The Performance Advantage
   (How do you outperform your highest expectations?) 73

6 The Recognition Advantage
   (How do you get your achievements noticed?) 89

7 The Advancement Advantage (How do you turn your
   accomplishments into career advancement?) 105

8 The Feedback Advantage
   (How do you know how you're *really* doing?) 125

9 The Awareness Advantage
   (How can you break through the bias?)   141

Conclusion: The Next Level—Balanced Leadership for
Better Business   159

Notes   171

Index   177

Foreword

Over the last 30 years, I have been fortunate to coach leaders at the highest levels, people who wield tremendous power within their organizations and in the wider world. Too few of them have been women.

That's because women are still a minority in C-suites and boardrooms, despite significant progress in gender equality over the last half century. Women leaders have done remarkable things (even as early as the 1970s, my great friend Frances Hesselbein was making waves as CEO of the Girl Scouts of the USA). But despite the notable exceptions, women too rarely advance into the top tier of leadership.

So what's holding them back? In this insightful book, Howard Morgan and Joelle Jay identify major challenges women face that keep them from both personal fulfillment and professional achievement. Even more importantly, they offer practical solutions, drawn from their long experience in executive coaching, to help women advance in their careers.

They begin by pointing to research showing that companies perform better with women in top leadership roles. This dovetails interestingly with my own research on 360-degree feedback—that is, feedback from bosses, peers, and other stakeholders. Statistically, I found, the average female leader gets better feedback than the average male leader. (That doesn't mean that all women are better than all men, it just means that women have a statistical edge.)

And yet women sometimes find it hard to capitalize on these advantages. For one thing, women tend to be hard on themselves, expecting perfection at work, at home, and elsewhere. When they fall short (which everyone does, sooner or later), too often they feel guilty. When I speak at conferences for women in leadership, this is perhaps the message that resonates most with audiences.

To these groups I like to tell a Buddhist parable about two monks walking by a stream. They see a woman crying; she needs to get to the other side without ruining her beautiful silk dress. The first monk picks her up and takes her across. The second monk is angry, because a taboo has been broken. Monks aren't supposed to go near women, let alone pick them up and carry them! The first monk says, "Ah well, things happen." The second monk continues berating his friend all the way home, and even wakes him up at night to tell him what a terrible sin he's committed.

"You should not have carried that woman!" the angry monk shouts.

"Oh her," says the sleepy monk. "I only carried her across the stream. You carried her all the way back to the monastery. In fact, you're carrying her right now."

Many professional women I've met find this message helpful. Whatever you've done wrong, leave it at the stream. If something or someone is upsetting you, leave them at the stream. At one of my seminars, a woman who is a very successful investment banker raised her hand and asked, "Could I please submerge them in the stream?"

Clearly, women face formidable obstacles, both internal and external—which Joelle and Howard can address with authority. Howard has been my friend and colleague for 30 years, and in that time we've authored two books and numerous articles together. We share a key philosophy when it comes to coaching leaders: instead of focusing on problems of the past, we both believe in setting a course for positive change in the future.

For 17 years, Howard was an executive in business and government, responsible for everything from mergers and acquisitions to start-ups to labor negotiations. He's been in the shoes of leaders who need to deliver results, which informs his coaching practice. As a coach, he has worked with executive teams, boards of directors, and leaders at some of the world's largest organizations. He's helped many executives make the best decisions for their organizations—and themselves—by aligning their mutual strengths.

Joelle is an award-winning executive coach, a keynote speaker, and the author of several books on personal leadership, including *The Inner Edge: The 10 Practices of Personal Leadership*, which has been used in leadership development programs in Fortune 500 companies such as MetLife, Microsoft, and Adobe.

She has helped many executive women advance through their organizations. She has also worked to make companies better places for women—notably through Leadership Circles™, a program based on her work. As a wife and mother of two sons, she knows firsthand the struggles of balancing work and family.

The 9 advantages that Joelle and Howard outline in this book are drawn from this wealth of personal and professional experience. They discuss how to handle feedback and get noticed for your work. They explain the importance of strong networks, for example, and of finding not just mentors but also powerful sponsors. With pragmatic insight, they discuss that elusive quality called "executive presence" that women sometimes need to make the leap to a top leadership position.

Rightly, they don't blame women for the dilemmas they face. The disadvantages and injustices women have experienced in the workplace are certainly not their fault! At the same time, Howard and Joelle urge women to take responsibility for finding solutions—to lead themselves toward a better future. If women drive change, they will be able to shape it to their own advantage. And they will be empowered by the process.

This book gives women—and men—useful tools to bring about that change.

—Marshall Goldsmith, leading executive coach,
leadership thinker, keynote speaker, and
author of 35 best-selling books, most recently
Triggers: Becoming the Person You Want to Be
(More information is available at marshallgoldsmith.com.)

He Said, She Said

Before diving into the main content of the book, we thought it might be helpful to provide some context for how this book came to be. A few years ago, we were talking and it seemed to us that the challenge of women moving into senior levels of organizations was making progress—unfortunately, probably at a rate and speed that would not satisfy any of us. We also looked at the materials that existed and while they were good, they tended to look at what was being done and provided an examination of what still was wrong. It was our view that the best solution was looking forward at what could be done in a progressive, intentional way to focus the attention on positive intent instead of everyone taking sides and avoiding the opportunity. After all, it is the opportunity that really matters. We have long believed that the greater the talent base of any organization, the better the possible succession solutions.

Organizations have always benefited from diversity of thought and talent. The goal is clear; the road has a little less clarity. Hopefully, our thoughts will help bring some of that clarity and help achieve the goal.

Now here are out personal thoughts on why we wanted to write this book:

Howard

Over my 40 plus years in corporations and consulting, I have had the privilege of working with hundreds, if not thousands, of talented, capable women. I have seen some receive the advancement they deserve and some not. Either way, it has not been an easy journey and I recognize that the challenges have outweighed the opportunities.

My experience is that most women have very little time to focus on themselves. They put a great deal of pressure on themselves to excel in both their professional and personal lives. In many ways, that results in them never having the time to focus totally on themselves and what they want and need. It is my hope that this book will help them have a focal point that permits some reflection, and more important, that it will provide some answers that will make it a little easier to find their balance.

The reason we approached the book this way is to help understand the perspectives on the major issues that women face. We have tried to build understanding of the issues from both a male and a female point of view. The purpose of this approach is to build understanding that will help all of us move forward a little bit more informed rather than avoiding the topic. In addition, while this book is written for women primarily, the hope is that it is equally helpful for men trying to better understand one of the greatest challenges of current leadership.

I apologize in advance if some of my thoughts are irritating. We wanted to find the balance of having an honest dialogue and not making the book so politically correct that we missed the opportunity to have a frank, honest review. My greatest hope is that the book creates the platform for moving us closer to where we all know and want to be. So, I thank Joelle and all of the senior women leaders I have had the privilege of working with. I have and will continue to learn from them.

Joelle

For me, this book started several years ago, when I was coaching a talented, committed executive woman—one of the leaders you'll meet in this book. She was highly focused on her business and is known for being an exceptional leader. She had a great reputation, was seen as a role model, and got consistently strong feedback. All good.

But there was another side to her experience that wasn't as good. At work, despite all the accolades, she felt like she could never get ahead. On the personal side, she was putting in such long hours that her health and well-being suffered. Most of the time, she loved her work and was excited about the future, but there was a side of her that was deeply discouraged.

Since then, I've observed the same pattern over and over in the women I've coached. Highly successful on one hand; exhausted and disheartened on the other. The benefit of executive coaching is it gives them a place to work that out. One on one, we have all the time we need to talk through their goals and aspirations, but also chip away at the obstacles and attend to the emotional side of being a woman in leadership. The impact is dramatic as women find their confidence, take ownership for their careers, and break through to higher levels of leadership. They are happier, more fulfilled. They find peace.

I want every woman to have that experience. I want women to be able to learn from each other *what works*. My intent in writing this book is to give you the advantage of having the strategies and successes of women who have overcome some of the toughest challenges of leadership, so that you can do that, too.

What I discovered is that this is a goal shared by many. It's been my privilege to work with Howard and all of the leaders who have shared their time and insight so we can expand our perspectives on the challenges and look for solutions.

For me, this is also a personal journey. As a mom with two kids, a busy home, and a full professional life, I, too, am finding my way. I'm learning along with you. I don't have all the answers, either, but I have faith in us to figure out. We'll do this together.

In Appreciation

We are grateful for the visionary men and women who have so generously helped us write this book. We know they'll continue to be an important part of the efforts to support women in leadership, and we thank them!

Introduction:
The New Advantage

"You are the promise for a more equal world. Lean way in . . ."[1]
—Sheryl Sandberg, COO of Facebook and author of *Lean In:*
Women, Work and the Will to Lead

Elizabeth

Elizabeth Keller was the senior vice president in a global role at a leading software company and the highest ranking woman in the company. Despite years of glowing reviews, accelerated promotions, and positive reinforcement, she felt she had finally gone as far as she could go. Her next promotion would put her onto the executive committee in a C-level role, but that promotion never came. She felt she had over performed on every measure she could think of and still wasn't given the job.

Finally, when she felt completely defeated, she gave up.

"I could see it was never going to happen for me at [my old company]," she said, "so I left."

When she left, Elizabeth's company lost a dedicated, talented, respected leader who could have done great things. Elizabeth felt she had to go somewhere else, even though she loved her company.

That's a lose–lose situation.

But that's not the end of Elizabeth's story. After Elizabeth left her company, she started over with a new perspective. She realized she could take ownership for her own career. She set out to understand the challenges she had faced and discover new ways to approach them—not as problems, but as opportunities. She engaged the leaders around her to advance women more successfully and create balanced leadership teams of both men and women. She eventually found her new role in a different company and is now the CEO—a visible success story and a role model for aspiring women.

Elizabeth learned what many women in leadership are learning: there is a great opportunity for themselves and their companies. That is a way for women to take the lead in their own careers and for their companies to support them in being successful. Together, they can advance women into leadership roles and serve their companies and clients better.

Now that's a win–win.

A better way.

A new advantage.

The Challenges for Women in Leadership

Women aren't advancing in business leadership as fast or as far as they'd like. Despite concerted efforts to crack the glass ceiling since the term first appeared 30 years ago, women have yet to break into the uppermost levels of leadership in their organizations. In America's top companies, only 4.6 percent of Fortune 500 CEO positions and 16.9 percent of corporate board positions are currently held by women—numbers that have hardly moved in a decade.[2]

Businesses want a better balance. They know their leadership teams need more women and they've heard companies with more women in leadership do better. Plus, they want their organizations to reflect the face of their customers. So many organizations have been trying, in good faith, to shore up the number of women in leadership roles. Dedicated efforts to attract, develop, and promote women are underway.

While that's hopeful information for women and a positive direction for companies, it's also surprising given the scarcity of companies that actually *have* such balanced leadership. Every year, the Fortune 500 companies spend at least $8 billion to promote workplace diversity, much of it aimed at advancing women, but with such little change in the makeup of corporate leadership, it clearly isn't working.

The problem for companies is they are losing out on valuable talent. Even where women start out succeeding in business, their numbers decline over time.

- Women represent 53 percent of new-hire jobs.
- The number of women at the mid-management level drops to 37 percent.

- The number of women at the vice president and senior management level sinks to 28 percent.
- The number of women in the C-suite shrinks again to 14 percent.
- The number dwindles to only 3–4 percent of the CEO positions in the Fortune 500—and even in the Fortune 1000.[3–5]

This persistent imbalance has real financial consequences. Companies with few women in leadership have been shown to underperform their competition by more than a third.[6]

It has personal consequences, too, for women who aspire to leadership. Women report being under unsustainable pressure and in some cases are tempted to give in or opt out, as the challenges for women seem intractable and companies seem impervious to change. The impact on businesses can be detrimental as they lose valuable talent and develop a reputation for being a poor place for women to grow their careers.

Of course, the advancement of executive women isn't just about promotion. There are other ways they want to succeed. Women want to excel in their roles and feel they are valued. They want to have meaningful work, strong and respectful relationships with coworkers, and financial security. They want to improve their salaries and be recognized for their efforts. At the same time, they want to enjoy their lives. In short, they want to be *themselves*.

If you're one of them, you want that for yourself. We want it for you, too. In this book, we will show you how to move from the same old dilemmas to a new way of thinking—one that leverages the gifts and talents of women, so they advance as leaders and discover new ways to succeed.

The New Advantage

As many companies are discovering, balancing leadership teams by leveraging the talents of both men and women has significant advantages—for companies and women themselves.

The Advantage for Business

Companies with the highest representation of women in senior management positions are known to perform the best.

The solution for companies that want to succeed in a competitive market is to take full advantage of *all* the potential in the organization—not just by advancing women, but also by optimizing talent across the company.

Reporters Claire Shipman and Katty Kay report in their research that "half a dozen global studies, conducted by the likes of Goldman Sachs and Columbia University, have found that companies employing women in large numbers outperform their competitors on every measure of profitability." For companies with more women, the results are exciting:

- **Companies with more women in leadership are more profitable.** A Pepperdine University study shows that the 25 Fortune 500 firms with the best record for promoting women to high positions are between 18 percent and 69 percent more profitable than the median F500 firms in their industries.[7]
- **Companies with more women in leadership are more competitive.** One *USA Today* report found that the stocks of the 13 Fortune 500 companies led by a woman for all of 2009 outperformed the S&P 500 (companies primarily led by men) by 25 percent.[8]
- **Companies with more women in leadership reflect the market.** Women are responsible for 85 percent of all consumer purchases in the United States and control nearly $20 trillion of the world's spending power.[9]

Companies with higher number of women at senior levels have shown results in

- increased revenues,
- reduced costs,
- greater innovation,
- increased employee engagement,
- higher productivity, and
- stronger leadership.[10–13]

In addition, the collaborative, more inclusive leadership styles attributed to women are more effective in today's team-oriented and global workplace.[14] Finally, in a marketplace where women make the majority of financial decisions, a balanced workforce more accurately reflects the customer base.[15]

Companies that see talent as a central part of their success strategy need to value the contributions of women and attain better balance among their leaders.

The Advantage for Women

We believe in the benefits of balanced leadership for business. Balanced leadership also benefits you. When women advance into leadership roles, they win in a number of ways:

- The opportunity to work with talented teams and people they respect.
- A sense that they are valued and contributing.
- A greater sense of fulfillment and satisfaction.
- Opportunities for growth and development.
- A sense of fairness in an organization that appreciates their talents.

All of this is important to a high quality of life—something women value along with salary and promotions.[16]

Women are in a position to empower themselves to advance as leaders. A change in perspective, a new set of strategies, and access to real, practical solutions are all available now more than ever before. We're figuring this out. After trying to have it all, be it all, and do it all, all the time—we have learned some lessons over the years about what works and what doesn't in advancing as business leaders while leading a happy, healthy life.

When the business world embraces the talents of women, when women are empowered to bring the full extent of their value to the workplace, and when women learn as individuals to make the most of the time and opportunities they have, then we will have achieved a better way of working—and a better way of life.

THE BUSINESS CASE FOR WOMEN IN LEADERSHIP

The successful businesses of the future will be those that attract, retain, and develop leaders from a rich and diverse talent pool at every level of the organization—from entry level positions to the board of directors. Significant advantages will benefit the companies that do.

Better financial performance. A study of the performance of more than 2,000 global companies over several years, ending in 2012, showed that companies with women on their boards had higher average returns on equity and higher growth.[17]

Improved organizational health. Research on the McKinsey Organizational Health Index found that companies with three or more women in executive committee level positions scored better than their peers on nine factors linked to well-functioning organizations. Companies that score comprehensively well on all nine metrics have shown superior financial performance.[18]

Global competitive advantage. In a global economy, the competition for talent is global, as well. The United States is being outperformed in the area of advancing women into senior leadership roles by countries such as China, India, and Brazil. Some of the countries taking more aggressive measures than the United States to improve their record with women include Norway, Spain, France, Italy, Iceland, Belgium, The Netherlands, Malaysia, and Australia.[19]

Responsiveness to stakeholders. The ability to reach a more diverse set of stakeholders is becoming an important goal for many companies. Given that women account for 85 percent of all consumer purchases in the United States, and over half of the workforce, women constitute an important subset of those stakeholders.[20]

Stronger leadership. The leadership attributes more commonly found among women leaders—including mentoring, relationship building, interpersonal skills, and collaboration—have been specifically shown to be more effective in a postcrisis world.[21]

What's Holding Women Back?

A number of obstacles have prevented the integration of women into the highest levels of leadership. First, change takes time. Second, few role models exist for women at the top. Third, we are still learning about the barriers that prevent women from breaking into C-level leadership. Two of the biggest breakthroughs in recent research for the advancement of women in leadership—*executive presence* and *sponsorship*—have only become prevalent topics of research in recent years. Finally, the historic reality is that, until recently, organizations were built for and existed for men. The business culture has been created by men as leaders, and characteristics associated with successful leadership are still aligned with more masculine traits.

Of course, all this is changing, and in some cases changing quickly. That doesn't help the extensive lists of motivated, high-achieving women stalled at the lower levels of leadership, waiting for the business culture to be transformed. If women want to accelerate the pace of positive change, they will have to play a leading role in making it happen.

Taking the Lead

As society and organizations continue to evolve, women who want to take their talent to the top will have to do things differently. They're going to have to take the lead.

There are four things leaders must do to promote the advancement of women in leadership for their companies and for themselves.

First, they must take ownership of their careers—what we call *personal leadership.*

Second, they must educate themselves about the old dilemmas that have challenged women for years.

Third, they must adopt a new perspective that allows them to discover new advantages available to them.

Fourth, they must engage the leaders around them—both men and women—in the effort. Women can take a leadership role in helping their companies balance their leadership teams—but they don't have to do it alone. Advancing women in leadership isn't a women's issue, it's a business issue, and requires a collaborative effort.

When leaders take these steps, they discover the new advantage of women in leadership and create win–wins for their companies and themselves.

Practicing Personal Leadership

In our work at the Leadership Research Institute (LRI), we focus on strengthening corporate leadership. In this book, we emphasize *personal* leadership.

Personal leadership is the leadership of the self.

- *Leadership* is the ability to define a compelling vision and inspire people to achieve it, by using effective strategies, systems, and solutions. *Personal leadership* is the ability to do that for yourself.
- *Personal* means "about you." *Leadership* means "going first." In a very positive way, personal leadership means putting yourself first.
- *Personal leadership* involves accepting responsibility, taking ownership, and applying influence to lead *yourself* to the vision you have in mind.[22]

Personal leadership is an approach well suited to high-achieving leaders. While human resource departments and organizational development teams try hard to help things go well for women, *only you* know what's right for you. You know where you're personally excelling and where you're falling short. You can define what success means to you and what you are (and aren't) willing to do to get it. You are the one who sets the vision.

As executive coaches who work with senior-level leaders in some of America's greatest companies, we spend our days helping leaders bring their personal best to their business. We will do the same for you. In this book, we coach you from the page, so you can do the inner work that brings out the best in you. By taking the approach of personal leadership, we give you the opportunity to find your own path to achievement as a leader. Personal leadership is a powerful approach to becoming a leader—and leading a life.

Understanding the Old Dilemmas

In the last several years, while coaching executive women, we began to see a trend. These were smart and dedicated women who were committed to the success of their businesses. They felt a sense of ownership, empowerment, and responsibility for their own success. They practiced personal leadership and were seeing results—but only to a point. Then they'd encounter a problem—some tough challenge they couldn't seem to solve. We call these the *dilemmas,* those impossible situations for which there are no obvious solutions.

Since then, we've interviewed more than 100 senior executives from international organizations on the topic—both women and men—and as we did, we discovered a pervasive frustration. As more than one executive put it, "I can't believe we're still talking about this, after all these years." We felt the same way. We set out to tackle the dilemmas.

We discovered that resolving the dilemmas requires an understanding not only of potential solutions but also of the dilemmas themselves. Throughout this book, we will describe the various ways women have been blocked, with the purpose of finding a new way forward.

We found the key in identifying the gifts and talents of women and seeing them as the secret to breaking through to new levels of leadership. We call these breakthroughs the *advantages:* the powerful ways women lead the way toward a better future.

Discovering the New Advantage

Here are the Nine Advantages for Women in Leadership.

1. **The Networking Advantage (How can you connect to influencers?)** Despite a reputation for developing strong and extensive relationships, women's networks are often less powerful than they could be. This chapter shows you how to strengthen and leverage your closest connections.

2. **The Balance Advantage (How can you succeed without the stress?)**
   Even the most high-achieving executives can be buried by the demands on their time, and this is especially true for women. This chapter gives you perspectives and strategies to balance your life so you can be successful and still take care of yourself and the ones you love.

3. **The Sponsorship Advantage (How can you acquire champions?)**
   Two critical relationships in a woman's network are their mentors and their sponsors. These partnerships have been shown to be among the most valuable in the careers of women for preparing them and advancing them into senior roles. We show you how to build them.

4. **The Executive Presence Advantage (How do you know you're perceived as a leader?)**
   Women are learning that being viewed as a leader takes more than great results. This chapter describes the elements of executive presence that are hard to define but essential to master.

5. **The Performance Advantage (How do you outperform your highest expectations?)**
   Performance is the entrance fee to a career as an executive, but performance means more than doing your job well. This chapter helps you see performance in a strategic way so you get the results you need to advance.

6. **The Recognition Advantage (How do you get your achievements noticed?)**
   Women who have strong performance, executive presence, and all the rest still have trouble getting their talents recognized. This chapter discusses how you can attract positive attention for your efforts.

7. **The Advancement Advantage (How do you turn your accomplishments into career advancement?)**
   Look at the rosters of any big company in the United States and you are likely to find a cluster of women stacked up in positions just below the top. This chapter shows you the trap doors in the glass ceiling, so you can move up.

8. **The Feedback Advantage (How do you know how you're *really* doing?)**
   Your ability to succeed should never be a mystery, and yet leaders are often missing good data on how well they're doing. This chapter shows you how to get honest feedback you can use to advance your career. Feedback takes the guesswork out of success.

9. **The Awareness Advantage (How can you break through the bias?)**
   When it comes to gender equality, most corporations are simply not there yet. In this chapter, we shine a light on some of the darker realities for women and offer solutions for creating a professional and acceptable business climate for everyone. Perhaps revealing some of the inexcusable situations women have experienced will end the complacency that allows these patterns to continue.

None of these topics are exclusive to women. All successful leaders have to achieve in these areas if they want to be leaders at the top of their organization. We take a look at the particulars of the old dilemmas that are problematic for women and see how they can be resolved to support women's promotability and personal success.

Cultivating a Balanced Perspective

Since we are encouraging balanced leadership in business, we offer this balance ourselves in this book. We've included a number of perspectives from both men and women—including ourselves, the experiences of our clients, and the leaders we've interviewed. We have seen in our work with organizations that this approach is essential to the advancement of women.

The Role of Women

When women have the chance to learn from other women, they gain from the opportunity to connect, share experiences, and work out the challenges they face—together. Women find inspiration and hope from other women. We find it especially helpful when senior leaders who are women can share the challenges and successes they've had, so future leaders can benefit from their lessons learned.

The Role of Men

Men bring something altogether different to the conversation. First, they lend important credibility and sponsorship to the efforts at advancing women. Second, they have a perspective on what it takes to succeed in corporate life that differs markedly from the experience of women and can provide insightful, contrasting views. Third, the interchange of perspectives *between* women and men when they both join the dialogue helps to shift thinking about what works in creating more balanced leadership. Without that shift, companies simply repeat the same old patterns.

Even though we wrote this book *to* women, it isn't just *for* women. These aren't "women's issues," and women aren't solely responsible for solving them. We have included men in the research and in the writing of this book, and we hope they will be equally involved in finding solutions to the dilemmas in their companies. As executive sponsors, managers, and peers of the women to whom we wrote this book, men play an instrumental role in their success.

About the Book

A few words of introduction before we begin.

In our roles as coaches and advisors to corporate executives, we help to identify the areas that have the greatest impact in helping talented leaders succeed. We may not be experts on every challenge you face, but we *are* experts in helping you think them through. We also don't always agree with each other, and you may not always agree with us. That's why, as we tackle the old dilemmas together, we don't pretend to have all the answers. But, we do hope to ask the right questions. We'll give you some things to think about it, debate some of the issues, and share our recommendations on the situations you may encounter. We'll help you discover your own answers, overcome the old dilemmas, and take advantage of the new opportunities that will lead to your success.

Who This Book Is For

We wrote this book for you—talented, high-achieving women who want to be their best and lead the lives they want to live.

In addition, we hope our discussion will be helpful for anyone who wants to contribute to better balance in the rosters of corporate leadership.

- **Executive Women.** Executive women leading organizations are particularly important in guiding the discussion. They've lived through these dilemmas. In some cases they've suffered through them. They've also succeeded. Executive women have powerful voices in the efforts to expand the success of women throughout the business world. We hope this book adds motivation, information, and encouragement for executive women who want to grow their numbers—whether that's you today or someone you aspire to be.
- **Executive Men.** Because they still hold the vast majority of powerful positions in corporate settings, the success of women in leadership is

accelerated with the involvement of men. We want men to take an active role in understanding how to advance talented women. It will improve their organizations, promote diversity, and increase results.

- **Leaders in Human Resources, Talent Management, and Leadership Development.** Executives in human resource roles have special influence in the development of balanced teams. They are uniquely positioned to institutionalize learning about gender and leadership. We hope the concepts in this book are useful springboards for dialogues at work, perhaps even generating ideas for formal programs and initiatives that will support the transformation of companies into places where all talent is valued.

- **Leaders in Diversity and Inclusion.** More and more organizations are focusing on diversity and inclusion. The executives leading in this area are charged with thinking about how to help businesses benefit from talent across the spectrum of all forms of diversity, including gender diversity. Our approach to identifying key dilemmas and discussing them from different points of view is a model we would like to see applied more broadly—for instance to help bridge gaps in generational, geographical, and cultural differences—to keep organizations moving toward a better balance with diversity of all kinds.

What You Can Expect

As we begin our journey together, let us give you a sense of what you can expect from your experience with this book.

Empowerment and Responsibility

We know you are not only talented, aspiring leaders, but you're also powerful women. You have important ideas for how to resolve your own challenges, and we know you have the ability to overcome them.

You will find in our discussions that we will be calling on you to challenge yourselves to make positive change. That means we'll ask you to take responsibility for your understanding of the problem and your role in the solution.

Please don't misunderstand us. We aren't saying the dilemmas are your fault. We are saying you can only change things when you take ownership for them. We will encourage you to look for opportunities to choose your thoughts and actions so you can find new ways out of the dilemmas where so many get stopped.

We don't want to take away from the tough realities you legitimately face. We do want to steer you away from unhelpful excuses.

A Lack of Blame and Judgment

Sometimes when discussions turn to women in leadership, women feel blamed. Frankly, so do men. We're not looking to blame anyone in this book, and we'd suggest you not, either.

We know there are men and women on extreme sides of the spectrum who don't help the situation, or help themselves. At their stereotypical worst, men can be blamed for bias and bad behavior, and women can be blamed for playing the victim. This is not helpful.

Our choice is to work with the men and women in the middle— well-intentioned, fair-minded people who want the best for each other and for their business. We'd ask the same of you. As you read this book, we encourage you to be aware of your reactions. Without blame or judgment, notice your reactions, and make a conscious decision to turn your thoughts in the most positive direction. That's where the answers can be found.

This book is not about blame. It's about choice.

Practical Advice

We hope you find this book full of practical advice so you not only understand the dilemmas better but also actually address them, successfully, in your own life.

As we write this book, the debate continues about why there aren't more women in leadership. Are women opting out of a high-powered career for a more balanced life? Do women take themselves out of the running for success too soon, and do they need to take responsibility for leaning into their careers? Is the business culture so intense and entrenched that women simply can't have it all? The debate is healthy but not always productive.

Our goal is not to stop the debate, but we do want to move *forward*. Join us. We invite you to challenge your assumptions, be open to various perspectives, and be willing to see new possibilities.

Meanwhile, you have a life to live. Part of the solution to the problem is much more personal than the media and online social networks suggest. You will find your own personal approach to turning dilemmas into advantages, and we will give you the tools to do it.

In Each Chapter

Each chapter will be structured in the following way.

- **A definition of the dilemma.** Each chapter begins with a definition of the dilemma so the issue is clear.
- **A description of the advantage.** We show you opportunities for resolving each dilemma with information, insight, and intention.
- **Real-life examples.** We share with you the inside stories of real businesswomen who have discovered the advantages. The examples are composites of executives we've personally coached—talented women just like you.
- **Expert advice.** We interviewed over 100 high-performing senior-level executives for this book from top-performing companies across the United States. Their experiences and insights helped determine the dilemmas and showed us how to resolve them. They offer their own experience as a way of helping you achieve your goals as they have done.

  In addition, we draw on insights from the research of academic experts and thought leaders. Their expertise, guidance, and wisdom can help you overcome the challenges with the best thinking on each of the topics.
- **Our perspectives.** We're familiar with the dilemmas because we've worked with leaders who have struggled to overcome them. We have spent our professional lives coaching executives one-on-one, in small groups, in large programs, and in global audiences in an effort to help them break through their toughest challenges and accelerate their success. We each take a turn in every chapter sharing our thoughts about women in leadership, based on what we've learned.
- **Q&A.** Each chapter contains a section where we wrestle with the common questions that tend to arise for each dilemma. We'll invite you into our discussion by sharing our authentic thinking as we, too, search for answers.
- **Key Points.** We summarize the key points of each chapter for easy reference.
- **Questions for reflection.** We know this book isn't the final word on these topics. We provide questions at the end of each chapter that you can use to continue your thinking and find your own answers for getting ahead.

Taking the First Step

You have the opportunity to look down the road now to see what's ahead. We have included a Self-Assessment you can use to measure your success-so-far in each of these areas. You may have mastered some of them already. Some may be entirely new. By looking at where you score yourself high and low, you can use this book to address the areas that will benefit you most.

Now, with a clear sense of purpose and the support of the extensive network of executives, experts, and thought leaders who have contributed to this book, let's explore the advantages available to you. Bring an open mind. Get ready to adopt some new perspectives and do things differently. By diving headlong into the challenges facing many women, you will find new opportunities for solving them and give yourself new advantage.

Key Points

1. Women aren't advancing in business leadership as fast or as far as they'd like.
2. Companies with few women in leadership have been shown to underperform their competition by more than a third.
3. Women are in a position to empower themselves to advance as leaders.
4. Companies with the highest representation of women in senior management positions are known to perform the best.
5. As society and organizations continue to evolve, women who want to take their talent to the top will have to do things differently. They're going to have to take the lead.

Questions for Reflection

1. What's your vision?
2. What are your goals? What are you hoping to achieve?
3. Which of The Nine Advantages for Women in Leadership present the best opportunity for you now?

THE NINE ADVANTAGES FOR WOMEN IN LEADERSHIP

A Self-Assessment

This survey will give you a sense of which of the advantages you have mastered and which ones challenge you most. Ask yourself, to what extent do I agree with each statement? Mark the corresponding number and give yourself an average score. Be sure to actually mark up your survey so you can revisit it later. A blank survey is available on the web site, www.TheNewAdvantageBook.com, for you to download anytime. Check in again every six to eight weeks. Is your score improving?

Strongly Disagree   **Agree**   **Strongly Agree**

Networking

1. I have a diverse and balanced network of people to support my success.

   1   2   3   4   5   6   7   8   9   10

2. I maintain strong, mutually beneficial relationships with the people in my network.

   1   2   3   4   5   6   7   8   9   10

Balance

3. I feel organized and in control. Everything I want to do fits neatly into my life.

   1   2   3   4   5   6   7   8   9   10

Mentoring and Sponsorship

4. I have mentors from whom I learn and who give me guidance, advice, and support.

   1   2   3   4   5   6   7   8   9   10

5. I have sponsors who are taking direct action steps to advance my career.

   1   2   3   4   5   6   7   8   9   10

Executive Presence

6. I am fully confident that others see me as a valuable and talented leader.

   1   2   3   4   5   6   7   8   9   10

7. I have assessed the impact I have on others and know it matches my intent.

   1   2   3   4   5   6   7   8   9   10

8. I get consistent feedback that I take the right approach.

   1   2   3   4   5   6   7   8   9   10

9. People respond to me as an equal—a professional that they respect.

   1   2   3   4   5   6   7   8   9   10

Performance

10. I know specifically what measures I need to track as evidence of my performance.

    1   2   3   4   5   6   7   8   9   10

11. I consistently deliver results in the areas for which I'm accountable.

    1   2   3   4   5   6   7   8   9   10

12. My performance exceeds expectations, as evidenced by my feedback and results.

    1   2   3   4   5   6   7   8   9   10

Recognition

13. I always feel like I have an equal voice and that others acknowledge my contribution.

    1   2   3   4   5   6   7   8   9   10

Advancement

14. I am pleased with the pace and quality with which my career is advancing.

    1   2   3   4   5   6   7   8   9   10

Feedback

15. I have requested and received high-quality feedback in the last 12 months.

    1   2   3   4   5   6   7   8   9   10

16. I have received feedback from all of the stakeholders in my career: my manager(s), peer(s), direct report(s), and my customers or clients.

    1   2   3   4   5   6   7   8   9   10

Awareness

17. I believe that others treat me equally and respectfully at all times.

    1   2   3   4   5   6   7   8   9   10

Questions for Reflection

18. What's your vision?
19. What are your goals? What are you hoping to achieve?
20. Which of The Nine Advantages present the best opportunity for you now?

CHAPTER 1

The Networking Advantage
(How do you connect to influencers?)

"By putting myself out there to help others, I've received in return. It's more a woman's way."

—Kathryn Tague, Assistant Vice President,
The Guardian Life Insurance Company of America

Tanya

Tanya stared at the form in front of her, stumped. As the head of a division in a scientific research organization, she had just been enrolled in a new leadership development program for talented women at her company. The first task was to get feedback from a number of coworkers who were important to her success. She had a few so far: her direct reports and some peers.

Tanya needed at least three more names, and these three were required to be leaders above her level who could give her meaningful feedback about her effectiveness as a leader. But who? Who did she know well enough to ask for that kind of input? More to the point . . . who knew her?

When Tanya realized she didn't even have three senior leaders at her company who could speak knowledgeably about her, she suddenly felt very disconnected. Who could she turn to for feedback? Who could give her insight and encouragement? Who would give her some advice?

One of the most consistent recommendations made to women who want to succeed is to *network*.

Like Tanya, many women haven't realized the benefits of networking, at least to its full potential, and they may be suffering consequences they didn't even realize. Without a strong network, you can be vulnerable in your organization. You might be missing out on critical information you need to do your job well. You could be losing valuable opportunities.

Forming a quality network takes thought. First, you'll want to build a network that's influential enough to be worth the effort. Second, and perhaps even harder, you'll need to find the time.

In this chapter, we'll look at the challenges that could hinder your networking and how to resolve them, so you'll be well connected to a network that fits neatly into your life. By thinking strategically about your network, you will leverage your relationship-building talents to create genuine, powerful connections with positive outcomes for business results—and for you.

The Networking Dilemma

Networking is about building strong, valuable relationships with people who help you be more effective. Your network is a vast web of connections, inside and outside your organization, of all your numerous and varied relationships, including clients you can turn to for business purposes, colleagues who can lend you career advice, partners with whom you can collaborate, friends with whom you can commiserate, talent you can draw on, senior leaders you hope will draw on you, role models, advisors, and more.

Most leaders know an extensive network is vital to a successful career, but challenges of networking can get in the way—some of which are specific to women. Even though women are known for their ability to connect and build relationships, their networks don't always work for them. Whether they are lacking influential relationships, don't feel they have the best occasions to network, or simply can't find the time, they can end up feeling disconnected. As a result, they may be left out of important information and opportunities.

Women are often told they don't network as effectively as men. Ironically, women are also known for building good relationships. Shouldn't networking come easily to women? What is it about women's networking that doesn't work? The women we've interviewed have their opinions:

- Networking takes time.
- Networking can be futile.
- Networking can feel forced.

They observed that their male counterparts didn't always seem to struggle with these same issues.

"Where do men go when they network?" asks Donna Morris, senior vice president, Global People & Places at Adobe. "They have golf courses, gyms and tennis clubs. Unfortunately the typical woman is spending her time running from one place to another juggling the demands of work, home and family."

Christine Morena, executive vice president of human resources at Saks, agrees and gives an example from her own life.

> Men form bonds in a different way than women. They will go out and drink together. They'll go to the ballgame together. Men will go to a meeting, and then they'll go to the meeting after the meeting. Women go to a meeting and go home. Recently a few of us [women] were walking out of the building and going to the train. It was 7:00 at night. We were all on a mission to get out! None of us would have said to each other, "Want to go for a drink?"

Networking is supposed to be the foundation for a solid career. For women to take advantage of the benefits, they need to approach it with their strengths, talents, and style and make it fit into their lives. Then they'll get the results they want.

If the old, traditional ways of networking don't work for you, then find one that does. Resolving the dilemmas around networking involves developing your strategy. You can redesign your networking around when you know who you meet, what you want to achieve, and how you want to connect. Then networking will work better for you.

The Networking Advantage

You gain the networking advantage by forming relationships that positively influence your careers, impact your results, and help you achieve your goals.

If your current approach isn't working, then a new way of networking is needed. As the way we interact with each other changes, so must the ways in which we network.

Research in networking reveals a number of trends that fall along gender lines. In networking:

- Women tend to lead with the relationship—developing it, building it, and nurturing it—but not always making the direct ask that would help them leverage the connection.

- Women tend to look for ways to give to others, but don't always exercise the opportunity to get what they need.

Men don't necessarily network *better,* but they do network *differently.* Compared to women:

- Men are task oriented and results driven, prioritizing business gains ahead of the relationship.
- Men are more comfortable asking for (and returning) a favor.

The founder and chairperson of the networking organization BNI summarizes the research this way:

- Women put relationships first, business second.
- Men put business first, relationships second.

Or, in his own words, "women find networking too salesy, and men find women don't take the business seriously."[1] If that's true, men end up with more business results and women with extensive relationships.

We're generalizing, of course. These observations about how men and women approach networking may not apply to you. The key is to find out what does. Understanding this simple contrast goes a long way toward understanding how men and women can expand their networks. When

Table 1.1   What Works in Women's Networking

What Works in Women's Networking	Where Women Can Do More
1. A holistic approach	1. A targeted approach
2. Interest in relationships and results	2. Emphasis on expectations and results
3. Connecting with others	3. Focusing on the business
4. Building relationships based on rapport	4. Assessing relationships based on benefit
5. Viewing networking as personal	5. Viewing networking as work
6. Getting support	6. Asking for the sale and closing the deal
7. Listening and empathy	7. Building credibility
8. Efficiency	8. Achieving goals
9. A personal touch	9. A business mindset
10. A diverse network	10. A powerful network

it works best, networking takes the best of both worlds—the relationship-building approach more common to women and the business orientation more common for men.

As women and men, we prefer our natural ways of acting and interacting because they're comfortable. But challenging ourselves to get out of our comfort zone and be more intentional in our networking can be the key to better results.

The Benefits of Networking

Many benefits come from developing a quality network.

- *Richer sources of information.* Different people offer different things—encouragement and safety from this one, the naked truth from that one, and a fighter who will stand up for you from someone else.
- *Multiple opportunities.* Through networking you put yourself in the path of opportunity. The people you interact with will point out (or even open up) a variety of avenues you can take to growing as a leader and accelerating your career.
- *Increased visibility.* By stepping up as someone who wants to connect, you begin to develop a reputation as someone to consider when opportunities arise.
- *Effective collaboration.* Working with people you know, love, and trust is one of the rewards of a fulfilling career. You'll feel less alone when you're well connected.

For all of these reasons, 93 percent of women and 90 percent of men agree that networking has played a role in their success.[2]

Our Perspectives

Howard

It's interesting to think that networking has become associated in some people's minds with bars and golf. That may be more of a perception than a reality. The truth is that networking is just as problematic for men as it is for women and for many of the same reasons. In fact, many of the executive women I have met are equal, if not better, networkers than men.

As you think about your approach, consider exploring new kinds of networking. Check to be sure your network is crossing the gender lines and including a variety of people so you gain from the diversity of perspectives and set greater goals so your efforts will be worth the time.

New Kinds of Networking

Given the changes in how we interact, in family, at work, and internationally, our ability to network is a way to stay current and build relationships that can be beneficial in both our personal and business lives. Networking is the number one area in which we interact, and it's just as important for men as for women.

It's important to recognize that as the way we interact with each other changes, so must the ways in which we network. Going to the bar, golfing with friends, and enjoying a business lunch happen sometimes but are probably not the key sources of networking relationships that are critical to success.

Let's take meeting for drinks, which is one approach people take to networking. It's also one of the least effective. What objective is accomplished by hunkering down over a beer? Escapism? When men feel threatened, they go to a place where they don't have to deal with the challenges. That's not necessarily networking.

Women have their own kind of escape. They may escape into friendships where they can just be themselves. When women feel threatened, they seek comfort and safety. That's not necessarily networking, either.

There's nothing wrong with a little downtime. But downtime is not the same as effective networking. One way out of the networking dilemma is to realize neither of these approaches is effective. There are much better ways to get results. When the right goals are in place, networking is far more effective whether it takes place in a bar, on the golf course, at a soccer game, on the phone, or at the kitchen counter. The key is to know the reason you're networking and spend the conversation getting that result.

Crossing the Gender Line

Another way to make sure networking time is valuable is to break out of the old patterns and form new relationships with both men and women. Men and women need to network with each other. It's critical today.

Networking can be self-limiting if women only network with women and men only network with men. How can the male-dominated ranks of leadership ever evolve if men never gain the perspectives of women? How can women break into higher levels of leadership if they neglect to collaborate with leaders who are men? Both men and women are better off when they look to each other for solutions and new perspectives on their challenges. There is an easy way to look at it—embrace the differences in genders and don't use them as a way of rationalizing the differences. When we do this, we gain the benefits of a broader, more diverse thought process.

It's more powerful to explore the many options for networking that will break open a broader spectrum of participants, topics, and outcomes. The form networking takes isn't nearly as important as the goal to stretch your thinking by diversifying your network.

Networking is essential. But it is not a gender issue. It's a task accomplishment issue. There's no more (or less) need for women to network than there is for men. There *is* a need for men and women to network effectively with each other and to do it in ways that work for everyone.

Clarifying the Goals of Networking

How do men and women make better use of networking to make sure it's time well spent? The key to success is having the right goals.

Consciously or unconsciously, many people go into networking with the wrong goals.

- "I'm going to hobnob and rub elbows so people want to promote me."
- "I'm going to get affirmation that what I'm doing is right."
- "I'm going to find other people to sympathize with my situation."

The right goals for networking are more valuable. Here are some examples:

- "I'm going to find people who help me be more effective in a given situation."
- "I'm going to find others who help me be proactive rather than reactive."
- "I'm going to understand more about the opportunities around me and where I can be the most impactful and successful."

Some people seem to be less structured and more informal in their ways of networking. Others find it helpful to be more structured and deliberate. Either way, the goals of networking have to be aligned to a valuable purpose for networking of any kind to be effective.

Joelle

Networking can be a perfectly natural part of your work life, especially if you connect with people well and stay in touch. However, if you want to be more proactive, you could take a more structured approach. You do this by asking yourself three questions:

1. What are my goals for networking?
2. Who can help me meet those goals?
3. How does networking fit into my life?

Questions like these give you the opportunity to design a process that works for you.

Three Steps to High-Quality Networking

1. What are my goals for networking?
Networking can serve so many functions. One way to streamline your networking activities is to be clear about the ones that are important to you now.

Let's brainstorm a list of reasons why you might be networking. Your connections can help you

- do your job more effectively,
- build strategic partnerships to accomplish big goals,
- influence others,
- gain visibility for yourself, your accomplishments, your ideas and your team,
- be aware of (and avoid being blindsided by) upcoming changes, decisions, and developments,
- understand the culture of a complex organization,
- shorten your learning curve,
- get advice and guidance,
- find quick answers to important questions,
- gain fresh perspectives,
- generate new ideas,
- learn about opportunities,
- access resources,
- connect to referrals,
- request endorsements for you, your position, or your initiatives,

- let others know how you add value and what you can do for them,
- develop business contacts,

and much, much more.

Give a moment's thought to what you want right now. What are you hoping to gain from being connected?

2. How does networking fit into my life?

Once you have your goals for networking, you come to the most important step: figuring out how to make it happen.

As we've discussed, the constraints of time and opportunity can conflict with your ability to network as much as or as effectively as you might like. If that's the case, design your efforts around the activities that work for you.

I often see businessmen and businesswomen dragging themselves to networking occasions late in the evening. ("I *have* to go to this networking thing . . . ugh . . .") If you go into networking feeling hassled and grumpy, you're not going to present your best self to others, and chances are you're not going to get much out of it.

Try this instead: Revisit your goals. Again, what are you trying to achieve? Now you can decide whether that same old networking event will help you achieve your goals or whether instead it's time for something new. If you're like many busy executives, you'll discover a wide variety of creative options that serve the purpose equally well.

Networking could involve:

- Meeting people one-on-one for planned and meaningful conversations.
- Having a regular conference call with a trusted mentor, sponsor, or peer.
- Attending industry events.
- Carving out a section of an existing agenda to connect more closely with colleagues.
- An impromptu phone conversation.
- Connecting online—via e-mail, professional chat groups, or social media.
- A standing meeting, a walking meeting, an e-mail exchange, or a walk down the hall.
- Starting conversations at work, on the train, during office hours, or on the fly.
- With social media, you can even network from home in your pajamas.

Of course, you're already having these conversations. You have them all the time. That's the secret—to suddenly see that all the work you do with people at every level of leadership is an opportunity to build a network. The difference between a random collection of contacts and a strong network of connections is not how many hands you shake. It's how many people you engage in a meaningful, mutually beneficial way.

However you choose to network, give yourself permission to be brief. By all means, if you delight in the company of others, spend more time with them, but don't feel you have to do that in every interaction. Focus instead on accomplishing the goal. If you can do that in the first 10 minutes of a half-hour meeting, you've bought back 20 minutes for your day.

For many busy executives, efficiency is paramount and networking can be as efficient as you make it.

Again, networking can be unstructured and informal, or structured and planned. Whether it's worth the effort is up to you.

3. Who can help me meet those goals?

Once you've clarified your goals for networking and thought about how it will look, you can better align your connections to meet those goals.

I once worked with an executive who was looking for a new role in her company. Tara's company had recently reorganized and she saw the potential to grow her career by taking a more instrumental position. Her goal for networking was to explore her opportunities with people she thought might be able to help.

Tara and I agreed to spend one of her executive coaching sessions designing her network around this goal. To get a sense of how well connected Tara was, we analyzed her current network.

All of the relationships she named were with people outside the company. Tara had made a common mistake—building a network of external contacts while neglecting important relationships at work.

"Who do you think could help you meet the goal of finding new opportunities *in* your company?" I asked.

Tara picked up her pen and started jotting down names. Executives in other divisions . . . her counterparts who had worked in other parts of the company . . . her new HR business partner.

In just a few minutes' time, Tara had aligned her network to what she wanted to achieve and knew where to build new relationships to her goal of finding an exciting new position.

What are your goals for networking now and what relationships will help you achieve them?

HOW TO MAKE THE ASK

Leaders can benefit from being more straightforward in their requests of their contacts and connections. Practice making the ask or defining your need—directly. Here are a few suggestions to get you thinking.

- "I have a goal of moving into a global role at some point in my career. Would you be willing to talk to me about how I can do that?"
- "It's important to me, in my role, to stay aligned to the vision of the company. Tell me, how can I be most helpful to you in being a leader that helps achieve that vision? Are there opportunities to get more involved?"
- "I know the company has layoffs planned for this year. I am a committed leader and a high performer, and I want to stay with the company as long as possible. Do I have your endorsement as a leader, and if not, what could I do to earn it?"
- "I am searching for career opportunities. I'd like to explore other positions in the company. Who could you introduce me to that might have an opening sometime in the next six months?"
- "I want to be more visible to senior leadership and get involved in some higher-profile projects. Will you put me on the new committee you're forming for the next big initiative?"
- "I need to hire a new chief of staff for our division. Who do you know that can send me a diverse candidate slate, so I don't have to start from scratch?"
- "I'm trying to get a better sense of the market value of my position. What do you think is the salary range for someone in a role like mine?"

Q&A with Howard and Joelle

I understand men and women network differently, but isn't it still true that men have more opportunity to spend time together on evenings and weekends, playing golf or having drinks?

Howard: A dose of reality may be in order here. Both men and women are guilty of making assumptions. Women assume men are all at the bar promoting each other and keeping women out. Men assume women are rushing home to their personal lives and ignoring their work. Neither one is true. None of my promotions has ever resulted from a bar or a golf course! And plenty of women I know are working—or networking— from home late into the evening.

Women, you would benefit no more by hanging out over drinks than men do. Men, you need to recognize there are more effective ways to network than golfing. Both women and men need to separate socializing and personal life from purposeful networking and make time for quality networking that build relationships and get results.

Joelle: I suspect those golf games and conversations at the bar have more influence than men want to admit. Women fear that the "male bonding" taking place in these down times turns into closer relationships that are rewarded when it comes time for advancement. Given the number of men promoted over women, you have to admit their theory makes sense. We might have to agree to disagree on that one. But I do see your point that golfing and bars may not be the old boys' club they seem.

Howard: Isn't there also "female bonding?" And remember women's ways of connecting might not be the bonding they seem, either! The activities are different but the outcome is the same: women's ways of working during work and socializing after hours with friends doesn't help them get connected any more than it helps those men at the bar.

Joelle: Actually, you make an important point. Men may (or may not) have golf clubs and bars, but women have book clubs, dinner groups, soccer games, parent-teacher meetings, and so on. I don't want to stereotype—men are involved in these groups, too. Men have informal networking groups and so do women.

One of the businesswomen we interviewed is a master at using these groups for networking. She doesn't just sit by the pool and watch her kids' swim meets. She assesses the parents, chooses who to get to know, and opens the conversation to business-related topics. Another woman we interviewed said she always gets to know both parents of her children's friends. ("I don't just talk to the mom I happen to be sitting next to at the concert or the football game. I get to know the dad, too. Voila, I've just doubled my new connection!") You don't have to be a parent to use the same technique. You could use the same strategy almost anywhere— on the chair lift at the ski resort, at a backyard barbeque, at the gym. Anywhere you go is an opportunity for networking.

Building networks this way has plenty of potential for increasing connections. It doesn't solve some of the issues we've discussed in the chapter. The size and support of your network are only the beginning. The power and purpose of your network are still critical.

I was surprised to hear you talk about women networking for "comfort." To me it's not about comfort, but connection. Does networking always have to challenge me?

Howard: It depends what your goal is. If your goal is comfort, that's okay. But if your goal is resolution, you're not going to find it in a comfortable relationship. Growth can be uncomfortable. Both women and men need relationships in their network that challenge them. If you have a question or an issue, you have to ask yourself, is my goal to commiserate and find solace with people I know are going to agree with me on this, or is it to get resolution? So be clear about the goals.

Joelle: In some cases, we need to push ourselves out of our box into experiences that challenge us to grow. At other times, we need to find a safe environment in which we can work through those challenges with people who will understand and support us.

What do you think of women's networking groups?

Joelle: I see value in connecting with like-minded communities. One of the reasons I like working with all-women groups is it gives them a place to work out the complexities of being a woman in a leadership position, and those challenges are sometimes different from a man's.

Howard: I'll give you that. But women shouldn't just network with women. They should also make sure there are men in that equation. Find someone you respect that's a man and help him help you advance your goals. Someone you trust. I can appreciate there may be value in women networking with each other, as well. But if you accept that point, then, you can't also criticize men going out to network together.

Joelle: That's true. Men and women can both have different kinds of networks for different kinds of goals. Your question also points to another key element of networking: the networking group. The benefit of a community environment is it brings more people in. The drawback is you may find yourself focusing more on their needs than your own. Finally, we should revisit the criticism that women's networking groups aren't always that powerful. It occurs to me that if men's networks—no matter how they're formed—include more powerful members, they are indeed likely to yield more bigger outcomes. Participating in a networking group may get you connected but won't necessarily get you results.

Both mixed-gender and gender-specific networking can be valuable, but for different reasons. Both one-on-one and group networking can be valuable, with different results.

I'm afraid I'm being misperceived as being uninterested in networking. Plus I'm not always sure I'm welcome anyway. It's easy to just give up and go home.

Joelle: Let's revisit the comment that men assume that because women are rushing home to their personal lives, they are disengaged or disinterested. Is that really true? Women want to be connected, they just find it hard to make room for networking on top of everything else in their lives. It cuts away at their confidence when they see men who seem all chummy and self-assured.

Howard: Just because men act confident doesn't mean they are, or that they have reason to be. Women may see men as acting more confident and feel less confident in themselves, when in reality the men actually look more confident than they feel.

Likewise, just because women may seem to be hiding out in their offices to get their work done or leaving work early to be with their families, it's not right to assume they're disengaged. In reality they are just working harder than ever to get everything done.

Joelle: That's a perspective shift, isn't it? Just because someone looks confident doesn't mean they are, and just because a woman has the right motivations for the way she is working doesn't mean she appears that way to others. There's a perception issue on both sides.

Howard: Exactly. Just as women misread the motives of men, men misread the motives of women.

Joelle: So the message for women is, find confidence in yourself as a leader, and be sure you actually are committed to connecting with others and building your reputation.

Howard: Right. Effective networking takes effort and commitment. Women (and men, for that matter) can attend to their home lives and also have a commitment to networking that fits into their time.

There's something about networking that strikes me as unsavory. It's so political. How can I build my network without playing the political game?

Howard: Networking is political. That doesn't mean it's a game. Political awareness is actually a form of emotional intelligence—a kind of empathy that comes from reading others' emotional currents and being mindful of power and relationships.

Joelle: That's an incredible reminder for women. Getting over the aversion to politics would go a long way toward freeing women to participate fully in networking.

Let's not ignore the connotation in the question, though—that networking-as-politics might be unseemly. You'll definitely want to avoid the perception of impropriety. It's always a good idea to be aware of appearances, but for the most part you can avoid the overly political side of business by focusing on the results you're after and choosing people in your network carefully. People understand the nature of a business relationship. Because that's what it is.

Tanya: The End of the Story

As she gathered names for a feedback process, Tanya had had an unsettling feeling. She could suddenly see how disconnected she had become from other leaders.

Tanya did a Network Analysis with her executive coach to understand the relationships she had and which ones were missing. Together, they created a new design for her networking—one that was strategic and intentional, structured so she could spend more time developing key relationships with people who would be supportive of her goals and aspirations.

Best of all, Tanya realized it wouldn't be that hard. She didn't need to make networking a big project to somehow squeeze onto her overflowing plate. She didn't need to set a networking goal or join a bunch of groups. She didn't even need to go to the bar after work. All she had to do was pay attention and make a little effort—something she already knew she did naturally well.

Now, she has a rich network of strong supporters—influencers and connectors who know her and with whom she has an active relationship. As a result, she not only feels more connected but she is also more engaged in the business and getting better results. Now networking isn't an imposition. It's an advantage.

Key Points

1. Networking is about building strong, valuable relationships with people who help you be more effective.
2. Even though women are known for their ability to connect and build relationships, their networks don't always work for them.

3. You gain the networking advantage by forming relationships that positively influence your careers, impact your results, and help you achieve your goals.
4. As the way we interact with each other changes, so must the ways in which we network.
5. Challenging ourselves to get out of our comfort zone and be more intentional in our networking can be the key to better results.

Questions for Reflection

1. Why is networking important to you? What are you trying to achieve?
2. Is your networking strategic or accidental? Proactive or reactive? Organic or planned?
3. Which networking strategies would be most effective for you, given your natural strengths and style? How and when would you fit those strategies into your life?
4. Which networking strategies are preferred by the people with whom you're trying to connect?
5. How many reasons *not* to network are false perceptions?
6. Who would be beneficial to include in your networking efforts?
7. What networking commitments are you willing to make?

CHAPTER 2

The Balance Advantage
(How do you succeed
without the stress?)

"I find balance in my career and family life, as both provide me with strength and opportunity. I manage them together."
—Christine Buscarino, Vice President, Office Depot, Inc.

Reagan

Reagan raced around the house gathering soccer gear and cradling her cell phone on her shoulder. Her team member at work, Steve, was on the other end of the call. Listening to Steve share his ideas about tomorrow's meeting with one ear and tracking her twins' efforts to get dressed with the other, she was the picture of multitasking.

"Yes, Steve, that's a good idea. Let's lead with the results from last quarter." *(Shin guards, cleats, jerseys—)*

(Whispering) "Boys, go find your socks!"

"I'm sorry, Steve. I'm trying to get us to a soccer game while I'm talking to you. Go on—*(Whispering)* "Everybody take your water bottle!"

Minutes later, sons in tow, Reagan zoomed to the car with her arms piled high. "Buckle up, everybody! Steve, I'll call you from the game and we'll finish our conversation." *(Snacks for the team, briefcase with my notes for the call with Steve, grocery list—remember to stop on the way home, oh and get gas, too—)*

"Everybody ready? You two eat your snacks . . ." *(. . . And I'll see if I can gather my thoughts before I call Steve back from the field . . .)*

For a fleeting moment as she pulled out of the driveway, Reagan was overcome with exhaustion. If only she could close her eyes for a moment. Maybe it wasn't possible to do everything she was trying to do at work and in her life, after all. Just as discouragement threatened to set in, she was yanked back to a vivid reality. Her phone started to ring and her sons called her name from the backseat.

"Mommy, what's for dinner?"

The second shift. The double life. Working two jobs. Run any of these phrases past a working woman—especially a working mom—and she'll know exactly what you mean. When it comes to succeeding at work and at home, many women feel they have to work twice as hard—because they often do.

The routine is familiar: get up early, put in a long day, work as hard as you can to make everything fit, wrap up as fast as you can, and race home to start all over again at your "second job" at home and in the rest of your life. You have to keep up the pace in every moment, and the speed and intensity can seem impossible to sustain.

But it *can* be done. You can sustain a healthy, happy way of life, be your best, achieve what you want to achieve, and not have to sacrifice your sanity or the ones you love to do it. In this chapter, you'll discover how other busy, successful, high-achieving leaders manage to balance their lives, so you can, too.

The Balance Dilemma

Balance means prioritizing the various elements of your life, with a sense of peace and confidence that you're making the right decisions for yourself, your career, and the people who matter most in your life.

The problem for busy leaders is there's simply too much to do. The pattern is familiar to most working adults in this fast-paced modern world: put in a jam-packed day at work and race off to a chock-full evening with family, friends, fitness, church, charities, personal goals, growth and learning, and hobbies. If you take on new roles at work—a promotion, an exciting opportunity, a big responsibility, and an important project—you risk dropping the balls in the rest of your life. If you don't expand your value at work, you risk professional growth and career success. You can't get everything done—but you can't *not* get everything done, either. It's exhausting.

What makes life especially intense for women are the roles they play in their personal lives.

- Ninety-two percent of women manage the lion's share of household tasks.
- Fifty percent of women do daily housework compared to 20 percent of men.
- Women provide more than twice as much care for their parents *and* their in-laws.
- Forty-four percent of women cite child care and elder care as reasons they leave their jobs compared to 12 percent of men.[1,2]

Many women feel they never get rest, as they rush headlong from their professional life into their evening work. Their jobs are never done.

Nita White, the executive vice president of Human Resources at Black-Berry, describes the situation as she sees it:

> Women still have to work twice as hard, I believe. Whether we actually admit it or not, women are still the ones who interrupt their career to handle the balance of life and family.

Another executive commented:

> I look at my male colleagues. Most of their wives don't work outside the home. We've come a long way, we say that things are equal, but you still have these dynamics in which women take the responsibility for managing a family's home life, whether or not they have a career of their own.

For women who wrestle with those dynamics, one option is to scale back their responsibilities at work to support their lives at home. Either that or they drive twice as hard to make it all happen, and in the process drive themselves into the ground.

And it's not just you who suffers. Your work suffers, too, and by extension, the business. The effects of prolonged stress on your effectiveness are profound. They include:

- a loss of perspective on the challenges that come up at work,
- an inability to look at problems creatively,
- the tendency to take workplace conflict personally,
- the exacerbation of negative personality traits, and
- a reversion to the status quo instead of increased progress and innovation.[3]

Constant stress doesn't just take a toll on your health, well-being, and mood. For leaders who want to perform at their peak, it actually limits your career, for the effects of stress work directly against the creative, thoughtful, attentive mindset you need to get ahead.

Even though your ability to manage the details of life is a personal matter, it's a business matter as well. When women lose their sense of balance, they tend to lose their ambition. In the research for *Womenomics*, Claire Shipman and Katty Kay found that "Work-life conflict is the top factor cited when 'high-potential, high-talent' women leave their jobs."[4] The pattern plays out time and again for many women in business: they become depleted and discouraged. Overwhelmed by the impossibility of doing it all, they finally stop trying. They slow down. They lean back. They opt out.

Fortunately there is another option. You don't have to pull back on your professional goals or pare back your ambitions. You can align your home life and your work life in a more effective way. You can make everything fit.

Resolving this dilemma requires three important things: a belief it can be done, a fresh perspective, and a few good, practical ideas for how to get better balance in your life.

IS WORK/LIFE BALANCE POSSIBLE?

Do you believe work/life balance is possible?

A recent Internet search on balance ("work/life balance is . . .") turned up the following responses, in order:

- A joke
- A myth
- Impossible.

These results reinforce a prevailing belief that work/life balance is unattainable. Maybe there's no such thing as work–life balance—only work–life choices. Maybe we should just be integrating our work into our life, not balancing them.

As a society, we seem to be wrestling with ourselves over whether we believe work/life balance is achievable, and if so, what it means. We want to be more balanced, but we can't seem to get more balanced, and if we can't get more balanced, then maybe balance isn't possible after all. But giving up on balance altogether doesn't seem right, because what's the alternative? To accept a life of stress and overwork? Many people are searching for an explanation that makes it possible to find a manageable way of living that seems harder and harder to find.

In this chapter, we use the word *balance,* because it's still the most common and efficient term we have to communicate the ability to attend to the different parts of your life while maintaining fulfillment and a sense of peace.

Second, we believe the metaphor works. Balance is the distribution of energy to maintain stability. Picture the yin and yang symbol. Yin and yang are complementary (not opposing) forces interacting to form a dynamic system in which the whole is greater than the parts. Just so with light and dark, high and low, hot and cold, and yes, life and work. The way you balance your life may be different than it is for someone else. You will still have to decide how to define balance for yourself. And you'll still have to figure out how to do it.

Balance *is* possible when you commit to understanding what "balance" means to you.

The Balance Advantage

The balance advantage starts with an open mindset. Yes, your life is full, but that's partly because you put such care and attention into all of the aspects of your life. That doesn't have to mean overwork and overwhelm; indeed it is the richness of life. So, if you wonder whether it's possible to balance your life, remember that, in many ways, you already are. You don't have to beat yourself up, constantly stressing about how you're ever going to do it all. You *are* doing it. Even now, you're reading this book to better yourself. You're accomplishing results in your career. You're holding your life together. We lead full lives. That's a blessing. Now we can devote ourselves to doing it better.

If you really want to know if it's possible to balance your life, just ask the people who do. You *can* have it all. You just have to know what your "all" is.

Luckily, solutions exist for all of us to get a better balance right now, if we commit to taking leadership in our lives. The same characteristics that make you an exceptional leader can be an advantage in balancing your life. That might include:

- Aligning your personal and professional vision.
- Being decisive about your priorities.
- Taking action planning seriously to create efficiencies.
- Getting clear about your strengths and values, and using them to maximize your time.
- Learning ever-better systems and building a personal support team around you to help you be successful.
- Committing to seeing new possibilities available to you when you keep an open mind about how it might be possible to have it all, all at once.

These are all practices of personal leadership leaders use to balance their priorities and reach their goals.[5] Many of our clients who lead extremely busy lives have been able to settle into a more present and peaceful mind-set by applying the skills and strategies that work so well in business—to themselves. It's amazing what you can do when you set your mind to it.

That's not to say you don't have forces working against you. High-profile decisions of women to leave senior executive or high-ranking government posts have highlighted the fact that many jobs, especially those at the highest level of leadership, are simply not structured to accommodate a balanced life. Nevertheless, we have more control over our time than we think.

To give one example, researchers found that by coaching executives to be more productive, they could save them hours and hours of time. The researchers taught the executives to think consciously about how they spent their time; decide which tasks mattered most to them and their organizations; and drop or outsource the rest, which resulted in a reduction in their involvement in low-value tasks. They reported that the executives

- cut desk work by an average of six hours a week,
- saved meeting time by an average of two hours a week, and
- freed up nearly a fifth of their time—an average of one full day a week.

They could then "focus on worthwhile tasks with the hours they saved." The same strategies that helped these executives "make time for the work that matters" can help *you* make more time for the things that matter in your life. Imagine you had one full day a week, to fill as you see fit. You could have time and energy for all of the parts of your life, so nothing has to be left behind. Perhaps balance does stand a chance, after all.

No one's saying reaching better balance is easy. The pressures of daily life in a nonstop, high-pressure, busy, global, competitive world—especially as a woman, and especially if you have children or other equally time-intensive priorities—can make it seem like balance isn't even possible. But it is.

With the right mindset, the right strategy, and the right information, you can enjoy your personal life and pursue your professional dreams.

The Benefits of Balance

The personal benefits of balance are intuitively clear. You'll feel good. You'll be happier and less stressed. Why?

1. You're more in control of your time.
2. You slow down, becoming more reflective and strategic.
3. You are able to optimize your time, so you're prioritizing the things that are most important to you and letting go the rest.
4. At home, you are able to get everything done and still have time for the joys of life.
5. At work, you are better able to think clearly, perform better, achieve your goals, and advance your career.
6. You feel more rested, relaxed, and energetic, and your company benefits from your effectiveness and results.

If all that sounds too good to be true, it may be because you haven't experienced it yet, but you will.

Your family and your work will also benefit. In their book *Getting to 50/50: How Working Couples Can Have It All by Sharing It All,* Sharon Meers and Joanna Strober conducted extensive reviews of the research on the effects when women work. They report that:

• Families benefit when women work.
• Businesses benefit from the talents of women when they can focus equally well both at work and at home.[6]

It seems a better balance is best for everyone.

Our Perspectives

Howard

It's interesting that women believe that men have an advantage by having a wife at home. I think that was true during my parent's generation. After all, my mother was forced out of her job on her wedding day because she needed to "free up" the job for a single woman who did not have a man to take care of her. We have come a long way. I think we need to recognize that the world, especially in North America, has grown to understand the changing home environment and value the important role women play in the workplace.

As you think about balancing your life, it can be helpful to recognize how important a healthy home life is for *all* people, men and women, and then to have the conversations at work and at home that protect it.

The Changing Home Environment

How the home and family obligations are handled has changed significantly over the last 50 years! I am not saying that it is where it should be or that it is as balanced as the responsibilities require. However, I think casting the "problem" as a gender issue may be avoiding part of the real issue. The home environment is changing and we need to change with it.

We need to understand there are more stay-at-home dads and same-sex home environments than there have been in the past. There are also a number of single parents in the workplace. I hear the same complaints from people who have the primary at-home responsibility, no matter which gender they are. Yes, taking care of the home side is a major responsibility. It is many times taken for granted. Many people, both men and women, want to be good partners and parents. They want their families to have a good life and to be as successful as possible.

I think many times this is an embarrassing conversation, and both genders are worried about the implications of even raising the topic. The major lesson organizations can learn is that raising a valuable and contributing member of our future society is critical. While still expecting people to be contributors at work, we need to recognize the changing home dynamic—one that is evolving away from traditional roles and division of labor, and toward one in which everyone shares the responsibilities. We need to ensure everyone has the flexibility they need to a stable home life.

Having the Conversation, At Work, About the Rest of Your Life

When it comes to gender, all of the positive momentum we have gained has come at a cost. It is now harder to talk about our family obligations. I believe both genders need to do a better job of being respectful of family and home lives. I also believe managers can do a better job of reducing assumptions about how people do their jobs, so they can manage their lives and still get the job done well.

One of the business leaders we interviewed is Peter Long, the CEO of the Blue Shield Foundation in San Francisco. He described his approach to working with women who were his direct reports:

> Three of the directors who report to me are women, and I've had conversations with all of them about their lives and their jobs. "What do you want?" I ask them. "Do you want to move up in this organization? What makes you feel successful? What are your goals?"

Simply by talking with the people reporting to him about what they want for their lives and careers, Peter is able to learn more about how to help them design the best strategy for their future.

What if your manager doesn't do that for you? You can initiate the conversation yourself. Even Peter said his efforts to support women in his organization would be improved if women could take the lead. As he said, "It would be super for more women to be honest about what they want and to be confident and clear about it."

When we elevate the importance of our home lives and be open to talking about how to work around them, we as men and women, managers and employees, team members and friends, can put our heads together to figure out how to do it all.

Having the Conversation, At Home, About Making Work Fit

I believe the first part of dealing with this dilemma is for partners to have an exhaustive conversation at home to develop mutual respect and understanding for each other. Many times, if only one partner is working, there is a lack of understanding and respect for how much effort and time it takes to tend to the responsibilities of home life.

Peter Long, the CEO who asks his employees what they want for their lives, also has those same conversations at home.

My wife is an MD. On occasion someone will make an unrealistic demand of her, like scheduling a meeting at 8:30. She's taking our kids to school at that time. Her first reaction is to feel guilty. ("I should be at that meeting! This is my boss/client/patient!") I coach her a lot on this to see if she can find a win/win solution for the meeting instead. ("What works for the kids, me, and also my boss/client patient?" and "Let's make it 9:30, so it works for both of us.")

Peter and his wife troubleshoot this way to make everything fit in their busy lives. The responsibility for balancing their lives is something Peter and his wife share.

I face the same type of work/family choices my wife does. I was on a committee that needed to do some work on a conference call, and the East Coast people set it up for 7:30 a.m. my time. I had to send an email saying, "I am still dropping off my children at that time. Please start without me." They laughed and said, "You're 'leaning in!'" I said, "No, I'm living." These are the same tradeoffs, and I'm the CEO!

Now, I do believe most men do not feel the same amount of guilt about going to work as women sometimes do, and many times, men look to the home as a respite rather than another equal part of our responsibilities. We men also are far more accommodating in handling a business matter that comes up, rather than heading to our child's ball game or relieving our partners so they can have their evening off with friends. Any good relationship requires respect for each other. Minimizing the other person's activities is disrespectful and demoralizing. The key takeaway should be that nothing gets resolved unless it is surfaced, talked about, and planned out. Think of it as developing a business plan at home.

Joelle

There are three directions from which we can come at the balance dilemma.

- **Beliefs.** Do you believe you *can* get everything done? Do you believe anyone can?
- **Mindsets.** How do you view your life, and could your mindset be part of the problem?
- **Ideas.** Perhaps the biggest breakthroughs in this area come from others' great ideas. Lots of people are busy in this life, and we're all

figuring out the tricks to getting things done. The bigger your bag of tricks, the easier your life becomes.

Let's spend some time looking in each of these directions.

Adopting Empowering Beliefs

Listen to the language around you, and you'll get the feeling *no one* believes they can balance their lives. People will greet you and say, "Hey, how's it going—busy, right?!" They'll call and say, "I'm sorry to bother you—I know you're busy!" They chase away their kids and say, "Not right now, son—I'm busy!" You may even say it to yourself: "I can't possibly (fill in the blank: go to the gym, see some friends, take an hour off)—I'm way too busy!" Coaches call these "limiting beliefs," because they limit the possibilities available to us before we even have the chance to consider them. Contrast those with "empowering beliefs," which empower you to be surprised by new alternatives.

The messages are so pervasive we may not even realize that busyness is actually a belief—not a fact.

> If you *believe* you're too busy to live your life, you won't.
> If you *believe* you can get everything done, you will.
> If you *believe* work/life balance is possible, it is.

In order to make this shift, you may have to suspend disbelief. But just because you haven't done something yet doesn't mean it can't be done. Just for the moment, imagine it's perfectly possible to design your life and make the decisions that bring you balance.

Mastering Your Mindset

There's no question the busyness can be stressful. You'll be much happier and at peace if you can find—and maintain—a positive mindset.

For example, take Sara. Sara is a 53-year-old executive whose parents are aging and need her more now than they once did. On top of having teenagers to manage and a husband with a time-intensive career, she has to be ready to run to the pharmacy for her dad's medication or take her mom to the doctor. For a time, she was stressed and short-tempered. As a senior vice president for a large division of a technology company, she had enough to handle with work alone. Then one day, stuck in traffic at the holidays, she caught herself blaming and complaining. Why was she the one who had to do all of this? Where was her brother? Why didn't her husband make more of an effort? Why wasn't her manager more sympathetic?

Then suddenly as she caught herself mumbling over her grievances, it occurred to her that she was grumbling about some of the most important people in her life. She realized how genuinely grateful she was to have parents she could help and kids that were hers to raise. She decided to embrace this sudden burst of gratitude. She realized for the short term, she would have to rise to the occasion. In a few short years, she might not be lucky enough anymore to have the opportunity to play such a central role in the lives of the family she loves.

Call it an attitude of gratitude. An appreciative mindset isn't just a mental trick. Focusing on the positive can change your experience. Suddenly all those "things to do" turn out to be the highest priorities of all.

Starting a Collection of Great Ideas

In the practical realities of daily life, your beliefs and mindset are only a start. At some point you need to know what to *do*.

Recently, I attended an employee networking group for corporate women at one of our client companies. During a discussion session, a group of about 10 women burst into brainstorming all of the ways they manage work and life. In about half an hour, the air was filled with solutions to some of the women's most toughest problems.

Here are a few examples:

- Be honest about what your job is, and what it isn't, then draw the boundaries so it doesn't overtake your life.
- Insist on an agenda for every call at work. You'll cut the meeting times in half.
- Invest in planning ahead. You'll have more control over your time and be less susceptible to other people's emergencies.
- Master the art of delegation. You don't have to *do* everything; just *lead* it.
- Be more succinct in meetings. Aim to get more done in less time, not to let a meeting fill an hour slot just out of habit.
- Send fewer e-mails. The fewer you send, the fewer you have to answer.
- Focus on the big picture and let the details take care of themselves.
- Give yourself permission to cut corners. At work, not every memo has to be a masterpiece. At home, paper plates and takeout food work wonders.

- Outsource! Hire someone to help with the aspects of your work that someone else can do—then apply that same strategy at home to off-load the laundry, cleaning, and grocery shopping. Do your banking and shopping online instead of running errands and set up automatic payments for your bills. You don't have to do everything personally to somehow have it all done.
- Swear off multitasking. Be at work when you're at work, be at home when you're at home, and practice putting down the technology to be with the people who are with you. Your stress level will drop and your focus will increase.

Some of these suggestions may fit for you and some may not. To open up the possibilities, start collecting ideas from the people *you* know. You're going to be astounded at the ingenious ways they practice the art of getting things done—and soon you'll be one of them too.

Now let's look at some examples from real-life executives who have found strategies to make the things that are most important to them fit into their lives. Think of them as images of the possible.

Collecting Images of the Possible

When it comes to believing, it's possible to get everything done, the breakthroughs for women often come from other successful women. Here are a few snapshots from real-life leaders showing how they live their lives.

- "My family comes first, and everyone knows it. I have been known to miss a board meeting for my kids. One day my assistant called me ten minutes before a team meeting and asked me if I was headed to my son's elementary school for a parent-teacher conference. 'You mean the conference I forgot about?' I said. 'Call into the team and let them know I won't be there!' I hung up and made a U-turn for the school."
- "When it comes to juggling my priorities, I think of glass balls and rubber balls. On an ongoing basis I need to keep all the balls in the air, but sometimes when it gets to be too much, I know I have to let some balls drop. I just make sure the ones that drop are the rubber balls. The glass balls are my top priority. Sometimes the glass balls are an important assignment at work; sometimes they're related to my husband and family; and sometimes they're a special project I'm working on. Those are the ones I protect."
- "I gave up running errands. It may sound luxurious, but really it's not. I pay my teenage son to run them for me. For the cost of a tank of gas

I can come home to a full fridge, the dry cleaning is in the closet, and a dog who has been to the vet. I can focus on what I need to focus on and he takes care of the rest."

If you want to believe it's possible to live a more balanced life, stock up on images of what it might be like from watching the women around you. Ask them for ideas. You'll not only start to believe it but you'll also end up with some great ideas for how you can do it yourself.

High-Achieving Men—Balance from a Different Angle

Breakthroughs about balance also often come from successful *men*. They may be just as busy as women, but somehow they seem to see the situation differently.

Here's just one illustration of how a telecommunications executive, who's a man, thinks about his life.

"I value my time. (Counting on his fingers:)

- I don't go to useless meetings. I need that time to think.
- I don't do other people's work. That's their job.
- I hardly answer emails. To me they're like junk mail.
- I don't do things just because other people ask. I have my own priorities.
- I have boundaries. When I'm not at work, I'm living my life.

I have clarity, and it streamlines things for me, in areas where I see other people struggle."

You may be able to hear in his voice that this gentleman isn't apologetic about his decisions, and he doesn't appear to feel any guilt. To embrace a new belief about whether you can get everything done, it can be helpful to listen to how men think about their lives. They really do have a different perspective.

All of these images of executives are just a tiny glimpse at the bigger picture of their lives. Are they also very busy people? Probably so. Do they also struggle with getting things done? Likely they do. But let's stay focused on the point. All of these executives believe they have control over their lives. They *choose* what they want to get done and communicate it to others. They empower themselves to make the decisions that are best for them.

You have to believe you have that same kind of control.

Challenging your belief system, adopting a new mindset, and expanding your ideas for making everything fit—these are just a few practical strategies that can help you balance your life. No doubt there are many, many more. Keep looking for the shortcuts, efficiencies, decisions, mindsets, and brilliant ideas that can simplify or streamline your life. Then you'll have time and energy to do all of the things that matter most to you.

TEN WAYS TO SAY NO

If you find yourself challenged in getting everything done, maybe it's time to stop trying. Women are famous for taking on too much. You will downsize your To Do list by learning to say no. Here are a few ideas.

1. **Share your real reason for saying no.**
   "I'm working on a special project right now. I'm afraid it doesn't leave much time for anything extra! I'm sorry, but I'll have to let this opportunity go by."
2. **Refer the opportunity you don't want to someone else.**
   "Right now my calendar is positively full! There's someone I'd like to introduce you to that might be able to help."
3. **Only offer what you can manage.**
   "I can't do that, but here's what I can do . . ."
4. **Postpone for another time.**
   "I'd like to be able to do that, but this time isn't possible for me. I hope we can try again!"
5. **Change your mind.**
   "I know I said I could meet with you today, but it turns out I won't be able to after all."
6. **Gracefully decline.**
   "Thank you for asking. As much as I would like, I won't be able to do that."
7. **Announce your decision.**
   "I wanted to share with you that I've decided not to take on any volunteer work this year."
8. **Set a time limit, and stick to it.**
   "I have ten minutes. What would you like to accomplish in that time?"

9. Remember: "No" is a complete sentence.
   "No."
10. Press delete.
   (Sometimes you don't have to answer at all. Literally or figuratively, just press delete.)

Q&A with Howard and Joelle

This issue of crazy-busyness seems to be getting worse and worse. How is it ever going to change?

Joelle: I worry we may be missing some of the issue here, or maybe there are multiple issues. There's the issue of whether women are respected at work and at home for their "double lives." There's the fact that it's not just women who lead double lives, it's also men, and really, anyone who has a full and complex life. Then there are the micro-level issues of not just how to manage work and home but the very concrete, daily details of pulling it off. Do we know what the root of the problem is, or are there many challenges running together?

Howard: A real solution is missed when we make this a gender-only issue. The real issue is all of us are now expected to be available for 18–20 hours a day. This is compounded when an organization operates globally. I think the solution lies with everyone involved. Organizations need to recognize the new reality, women need to look for workable solutions, and men need to be supportive and participate.

How do you get your boss to support you in getting everything done—and not to be part of the problem?

Joelle: I see tremendous value in the conversations you've recommended, at work and at home. In my view, people are sorely lacking in the courage or confidence or skill to take these conversations on, but they may be the best course out of the conundrum.

One of the companies where we've seen this work uses a tool they call Work/Life Balance Plans. Employees use the template to define what they need to balance their priorities, and then they share those with their managers and teams. You don't have to work at a company with Work/Life Balance Plans to make this work for you. Just borrow the model. Give thought to what you need to be highly successful at work—including fitting it into a schedule that allows you to lead the rest of your life—and share it. Then ask other people to share their needs with you. Everyone needs balance, and if we have this conversation, people will manage their expectations differently of each other and themselves. This takes away some of the misconceptions (on one side) and the guilt (on the other) and replaces them with compassion, connection, understanding, and a better environment at work.

Howard: One of the problems with feeling guilty or embarrassed is we tend to avoid the problem and therefore, the solution. Things that are awkward do not get fixed—they just become more divisive to everyone involved. We have made this subject very difficult to talk about both at work and at home. It only becomes more of an irritant and never gets resolved.

Like many things in life, there is a compromise here. What we need to do is to reduce our stress in having the conversation. People have to be engaged to be highly productive. If they do not feel their contribution is valued or appreciated, there will be problems.

I feel like when it comes to work/life balance, I'm trapped. No matter what decision I make, I have to sacrifice something. How do I get ahead without giving anything up?

Joelle: I mentioned earlier that one way out of the balance dilemma is to take control of your own life—but that doesn't meant there aren't consequences to the decisions you make. Many women do give things up, as do men. So far, our modern world has done a poor job making balance a priority. Some executives forgo marriage and children to focus on their career. Some miss what amounts to years with their families, and some trim back their careers to raise their families instead. We should get away from the idea that every role can or should be equally manageable for everyone at any stage of life.

Earlier we brought up Peter Long as one leader who had insight to share about how to have the conversations that help people get everything done, but there's a pretty important other side to that reality that we should admit. Peter once joked with me about the effect of his family's focus on kids. "It's important to us to spend time with the kids. We've made a decision to be child-focused. If we didn't, we'd own a better house!"

By choosing to live a family-focused life, Peter has chosen not to pursue a more intense and potentially more lucrative career path. In much the same way, someone who chooses a very healthy work/life balance may sacrifice some time-consuming career-advancing opportunities. Someone who chooses the 24/7 work style may conversely lose something on the side of personal life. I once interviewed a famous author who, reflecting on her celebrity status and rewarding career, shared that on the flip side she had given up her personal friendships. Every decision is a tradeoff.

Whenever we make a decision about how we are going to live our lives, we need to recognize the consequences of our decisions and be sure they're congruent with what we want for our lives.

Howard: You're right. If we make a decision, we need to honor it or change it. There is not an option of continually complaining about it. If conditions have changed from when you make the decision, change the decision. We cannot always get what we want—but we can always make a choice.

Do you think the pressures of getting everything done hold women back?

Joelle: In my coaching of executive women, I have observed many instances of women legitimately feeling held back by their life choices.

There's the executive who by every account—including her boss's— should be playing an international role in her very large global company, but simply can't because the headquarters would require her to move her family to a new city, and she doesn't want to uproot her kids' lives and change their schools.

There's the group of top-earning saleswomen who are held back in their positions and cannot break into any kind of management role, because the company has structured those management positions to require endless travel and evening engagements that conflict with obligations at home.

There's the general manager who wants to stay in her division and be the very best GM to ever hold the position, who is committed to the company's success and sees it as the perfect job for her, where she can be the most senior executive in the area of the company where she lives and where her kids go to school—but who has received definitive remarks from the men who would advance her that "if all you want to do is stay put and not grow, you're not worth any further investment."

How do women who want to advance fight the established organizational decisions that contradict their goals for themselves?

Howard: Every time someone brings this up, I think back to some work that I did at an organization years ago. To its credit, this company was as early adopter in understanding the necessity for organizations to tackle the matter of feeling held back. We ended up developing an operating philosophy of "What you get out of your job will be commensurate with what you put into it."

I am the first to agree that many times women make family choices that make it very difficult to have the flexibility to certain assignments.

However, I believe the world has changed, and candidly, in a dual working parent household, this could happen to either parent—and it has. I know a number of senior female leaders that were the primary money providers in their family. When asked to move, they accepted and their husbands found themselves without the ability to work in the new country.

Now, I am not saying there are no backward thinking bosses out there. However the issue of uprooting a family to move can apply to anyone. If a man says he is not willing to move, many times, it can be taken even more negatively. For men, it can be viewed as an act of betrayal. So, for me, the real issue is whether both partners are willing to undertake what is required to move ahead. If not, that is okay. For those of us that travel frequently, it would be great to not have to do the endless travel and evening engagements. But if it is part of the job, we have to decide if it's a job we want. If it is, we need to respect the consequences.

Joelle: I like to think we are the ones who decide for ourselves whether a decision is right for us and fits with our time and commitments. In *Getting to 50/50*, Meers and Strober point out that our circumstances sometimes work against us. They discovered many women who felt "caught in a vise—between husbands who weren't doing their share at home and bosses who wouldn't give an inch at work." Even in the most inflexible circumstances, somewhere within that situation there is still a choice—to stay or to move on, to propose a different way of doing things, to accept a certain reality or to persist in making a change. We sometimes have more power than we think.

Reagan: The End of the Story

Reagan was a promising leader with a bright future, but she was just about ready to walk away. Maybe she should leave her job and focus on her family, at least until her kids were grown.

Then she realized she loved her job and wanted to see how far she could go. If only she could do both.

Reagan understood no one else could get her out of this predicament but herself. She took leadership of the situation. She developed a strategy—a Personal Strategic Plan—to make everything fit. With creativity, planning, and resourcefulness, she was able to identify clearly what she really wanted for her life—at home, in her career, and for herself. She gathered plenty of ideas from leaders she knew—both men and women—about how to make everything fit, resulting in an extensive collection of solutions for balancing work and life.

When Reagan could see how her life could fit together on paper with more time for her and less stress at work, she had a new sense of hope. And that is how, year after year, Reagan has moved from vice president to senior vice president to executive vice president of her company—without sacrificing herself, her sanity, or quality of life with the ones she loves.

Now instead of feeling at a disadvantage compared to colleagues of hers who, by luck or by choice or by stage of life, seemed to have more time to devote to their careers, she felt extremely fortunate. She knew what she wanted out of life and was working toward it. Indeed, it was already hers.

Key Points

1. If you take on new roles at work, you risk dropping the balls in the rest of your life. If you don't expand your value at work, you risk professional growth and career success. You can't get everything done—but you can't *not* get everything done, either.
2. Constant stress doesn't just take a toll on your health, well-being, and mood. It actually limits your career.
3. When women lose their sense of balance, they tend to lose their ambition.
4. If you really want to know if it's possible to balance your life, just ask the people who do. You can have it all. You just have to know what your all is.
5. With the right mindset, the right strategy, and the right information, you can enjoy your personal life and pursue your professional dreams.

Questions for Reflection

1. What's important to you at home? What's important to you at work? Do you see any potential conflicts? How might your answers change in five years?
2. Where, specifically, do you find it difficult to balance your life? How might you be able to restructure responsibilities, outsource tasks, or let things go to make it all fit?
3. Where do you need to assert yourself differently?
4. What conversations do you need to have to ease the state of overbusyness?
5. What new ways of thinking about balance and busyness will help you move toward a more balanced life?

CHAPTER 3

The Sponsorship Advantage
(How do you acquire champions?)

"The willingness of people to advocate for you really is the largest driver of growth, stretch and opportunity."
—Annalisa Jenkins, President and CEO,
Dimension Therapeutics

Melissa

Melissa looked like a woman with confidence. An elegant woman with a self-assured stride, she could walk into a room and command attention. When she stood still, people gathered around her. When she spoke, they listened.

That was on the outside.

On the inside, Melissa felt less secure. The general manager for a division of a leading software company, she had plenty of responsibility, credibility, and experience, but for some reason she was never sure it was enough.

"With my clients and business partners, I feel fine," she explained. "Where I start to get nervous is when I'm in a bigger forum with senior leadership. I really panic around our CEO! He is a force of nature, and he demands a lot of the people around him. I'm always afraid I'm going to get called out. I feel like I have to prove myself. Maybe I lack confidence. Whenever they talk about tough issues I try to disappear into the wallpaper. It's the area I struggle with most."

Even though Melissa could point to evidence she was valued (or at least, she had no reason to believe otherwise), she couldn't shake the feeling she was on the fringe of the leadership team. "Do I just assume everything

is fine? Do keep soldiering on? Or am I becoming irrelevant?" she won-
dered. "Sometimes I wonder why I'm here."

Even though Melissa sometimes doubted herself in the boardroom, she knew she was qualified as a leader. She trusted her own business decisions and had a good track record. What she didn't have was validation—a guide or a partner to confirm she was on the right track. As one of few women in a heavily male-dominated field, she felt vulnerable and unsure of whether her career would continue to accelerate.

Her experience is familiar for many women. You think you're valued in your organization. But who can tell? Your boss is absorbed in his or her own career. No one else is focused on you. If you're not careful, you start to wonder if you're important after all. It's a tenuous place to be, alone at the top of the organization with no one ready to defend you. No one to champion you. No one lobbying on your behalf.

The lack of evidence that they are valued in their companies can actually lead women to lower their ambitions for themselves and trigger a downward turn in their careers.[1] Don't let that happen to you.

You can become connected to a powerful lifeline. In this chapter, we talk about how to get mentors and sponsors who can help you sustain the confidence and momentum it takes to succeed and who can pave the way for future success. That's more than just beneficial. It's necessary.

The Sponsorship Dilemma

In order to build strong mentoring and sponsoring relationships, we need to distinguish clearly between the two.

> A *mentor* is a guide who offers you advice, helps you solve prob-
> lems, provides a sounding board, and shares his or her years of expe-
> rience to help you learn and grow.
> A *sponsor* is a powerfully positioned champion who advocates
> for you, opens the door to new opportunities for you, introduces
> you to the right people, increases your visibility, and makes the case
> for your advancement.

Mentoring is taking an interest *in* you. Sponsorship is taking action *for* you.

Leaders are advised to have a mentor, and many of them do. But is it *enough?* That's the question posed by Sylvia Ann Hewlett, the CEO of the Center for Talent Innovation. Her research with well over 3,000 executives revealed that leaders don't just need a mentor. They need a sponsor.

Sponsorship turns out to be critical for all leaders. The trouble is it's less accessible to women. Only 13 percent of full-time female employees at large companies have sponsors or colleagues senior enough to make a career-changing impact with their support compared to 46 percent of men.[2]

There are several reasons women lack sponsors.

- Women may not have recognized the distinction between mentors and sponsors and the need to build both of these kinds of relationships.
- Women may have thought the mentors they did have provided all the support they needed.
- Women may not have ready sponsors, as men are shown to have more sponsors than women.
- Women may neglect to take full advantage of the relationships they do have.

To this last point, a number of obstacles can prevent women from getting sponsorship, such as the hesitancy to ask for help or showcase their own talents; real or imagined boundaries across power relationships; the tendency to underreach for promotions; and sometimes even fears about what others might think. As a result, even women who do have a healthy network can end up over-mentored and under-sponsored.

Women can find themselves isolated—aware they need powerful relationships but missing the connections to secure them. As a result, they end up vulnerable—lacking support and advocacy at a critical point in their career.

Once you know you need a mentor *and* a sponsor, you can form those relationships and take advantage of all they have to offer.

The Sponsorship Advantage

As an integral part of your network, your mentorships and sponsorships are deeper, more focused relationships that deserve special attention.

The Value of Mentors

Mentorship gives leaders a distinct advantage. From protégés and apprentices to student teachers, law clerks, medical interns, and more, generations of leaders have benefited from the long and cherished tradition of mentoring. The mentorship advantage shortens the learning curve, provides support in a challenging time, and offers a way to learn the nuances that lead to mastery in a skill—not to mention it can be the foundation for a lifelong relationship, often treasured on both sides.

Mentorships can be invaluable because they are familiar and safe. You need a place to be yourself. You need the people who let you make mistakes and steer you right, with understanding and a lack of judgment. You can learn and grow with little risk.

So by all means, spend time with your mentors, but also remember the purpose. Your mentors help you do well, but if you also want to advance, you'll need a sponsor.

The Necessity of Sponsors

Identifying the need for sponsorship and differentiating it from mentoring have been a major contribution for women as they strive to achieve greater career advancement. They can now build for themselves the kind of backing that, presumably, men have always had. The sponsorship advantage gives women the chance to stretch beyond their own boundaries into opportunities they may not have had otherwise.

In *The Sponsor Effect: Breaking Through the Last Glass Ceiling*,[3] Hewlett recommends that aspiring women include not just mentors but also powerful sponsors in their networks. Referring to some of the most accomplished women in business, the report says,

> Behind every one of these highly visible women you'll find a powerful backer, usually male, who so believes in his protégé that he's put his own reputation on the line to promote her all the way up to the top. . . . The firepower of such a network is measurable. With it, the ambitious and highly qualified make it to senior-most executive suite, no matter how stiff the headwinds. Without it, they languish in the lowers echelons of power no matter how hard they work and no matter how well they perform.

When women have a sponsor, the likelihood that they will seek other ways of advancing their career, such as a stretch assignment or a raise, goes up 8 percent—a small but significant impact.

For that reason, companies are instituting programs to facilitate sponsorship. Nearly a third of *Working Mother*'s Best 100 Companies report having some kind of sponsorship program for women. One study even showed that women who found mentors through formal programs were 50 percent more likely to be promoted than those who found their own mentors, so the evidence points to positive results from these efforts.[4]

Even if you don't have that advantage at your own organization, you can learn to create those relationships for yourself. Annalisa Jenkins, president and CEO of Dimension Therapeutics, described to us how she strategized to find her sponsors.

"I need to know what's important to the people advocating for me. Why should they support me? Do they think they are potential sponsors for me, and why? What do I need to do to help them to be an effective advocate for me?"

When leaders have strong mentors and sponsors in place, they feel supported and championed. Women in leadership must educate themselves about the benefits of mentors and sponsors, fill those roles, and cultivate and leverage the relationships. That's what they're for.

Through the challenges of business leadership, you will find reassurance and support from your mentor. Complement that with a strong, proactive sponsor—a senior leader who actively takes steps on your behalf—and you can count on your chances to move onward and upward through a successful career.

The Role of Men in the Promotion of Women

As you consider your mentors and sponsors, be aware that men and women bring different strengths to these relationships.

Women are often drawn to other women for these roles. Perhaps they find it safe, or perhaps they see themselves in these accomplished women and find it inspiring to follow in their footsteps. These are valuable aspects of women's relationships with other accomplished women and hold special meaning. These are relationships to develop and preserve.

Table 3.1 Valued Mentors, Powerful Sponsors

	Mentors	Sponsors
Why they matter	Mentors guide and advise you.	Sponsors champion and advance you.
Who they are	Mentors are valued teachers and more experienced counterparts who want to see you succeed.	Sponsors are senior-ranking executives with power and influence that agree to publicly attest to your value.
How they help	Mentors teach you, guide your learning, offer a sounding board, talk with you, and encourage you.	Sponsors endorse you, advise you, expand your vision of yourself, talk about you, and promote you.

(continued)

Table 3.1 Continued

	Mentors	Sponsors
What they do	• Share their wisdom and experience. • Help you work through your challenges. • Work with you to overcome obstacles.	• Make you visible to leaders within the company. • Overperform with exceptional results. • Open doors to promotion after promotion—all the way to the top.
What you do	Your job is to: • Learn. • Grow. • Apply the learning. • Value and maintain the relationship. • Pay it forward by mentoring others.	Your job is to: • Prove you're worth the time, effort, and credit. • Make your sponsor look good. • Take on responsibility. • Arrange frequent ongoing meetings with your sponsor.
Challenges to overcome	As supportive as they can be, mentors don't necessarily influence outcomes in your career.	Because of the influential nature of the relationship, you may only want to expose your sponsor to your strengths and successes—even when you need learning and support.
	With so few women role models, mentors can be few and far between, and those who do mentor others can be overwhelmed with requests.	Senior-level executives can be extremely busy, and they also need to protect their own jobs and reputation.

The problem is that if your mentor or sponsor is a woman, even if she is the highest ranking woman in the entire company, the odds are overwhelming that she is outranked by other men, and when it comes to promoting the advancement of women she may be the weakest voice in the room. According to many women who have raised the importance of balanced leadership with their executive peers, she may be the *only* voice advocating for women at the table.

Men also play an important role in the mentoring and sponsorship of women. Men hold more positions of power and influence, and they are acutely attuned to a business culture that has historically been built around men. They can provide a different point of view and navigate the systems and decisions that advance your career.

Men who willingly take on this role can improve corporate leadership and results by helping to balance talent at the senior level. By lending their voices and their votes to the promotion of women, they are changing the face of organizations—an effort that by all accounts leads to better business.

The leaders we've worked with who have been sponsored by men express great appreciation for the commitment their sponsors have made, recognizing that as a result of the relationship, their careers advanced further and faster. As Annalisa Jenkins told us, "I am clearly where I am today because of the men who saw something I often could not see, and who pushed me forward and opened the doors of opportunity. I have always tried to make them proud and to feel I would become part of their own professional legacy."

No doubt there are many successful executives of either gender who thoughtfully seek diversity at every level of their organization and are working hard to promote both women and men. But the practical truth (and the research) suggests that biases still exist—even unconsciously— that make it necessary for women to have powerful backing. Women who want to move up must think about their sponsors not just in terms of who gives the best advice but also where the power lies.

The Benefits of Mentors and Sponsors

Even if you intuitively believe in the value of mentors and sponsors, the relationships take effort. Without a strong commitment on your part, they can easily fall to the bottom of a long list of things you could be doing to advance your career.

For extra motivation, consider the results.

- Women who take advantage of mentoring opportunities maintain their ambition and self-confidence in their careers.[5]
- People who are mentored "garner more promotions, higher salaries, and more career satisfaction and even report being less stressed than those who lack such guidance."[6]
- With the benefit of a sponsor, the likelihood goes up significantly of either a man or a woman asking a manager for a raise, an assignment to a high-visibility team, or a plum project.[7]
- Men and women with sponsors are most satisfied with their career advancement. In this regard, they obtain a "sponsor effect" from 19

to 23 percent. The benefits are even more impressive for mothers, at 27 percent, and minorities, up to 65 percent.[8]

The message is to develop both mentors and your sponsors, have several of both, and differentiate between the roles they play in your career. When you do, you will be surrounded by opportunities where you can add value and gain benefits in return.

Our Perspectives

Howard

In mentoring and sponsorship, three conditions contribute to lasting and effective relationships: reciprocity, chemistry, and mutual benefit.

Reciprocity

The first condition to create in your relationships is reciprocity. Mentorships and sponsorships work most effectively when they are reciprocal. It's true of most things in life.

If one person has helped and contributed a lot, and there's nothing coming back, then at some point the relationship starts to strain and wane. It doesn't have to be equal, but it can't be one sided.

One way you can contribute to the relationship is to make it easy. Your mentor or sponsor will bring his or her time, attention, and expertise. You bring the rest. Here are 10 ways you can support the development of your relationship with your mentor or sponsor.

1. Request the time when you need it and organize the meeting time.
2. Design the agenda.
3. Choose your questions.
4. Identify the outcomes.
5. Show your progress.
6. Listen.
7. Propose next steps.
8. Develop a point of view.
9. Exercise initiative and participate in your own progress.
10. Overachieve on your goals.

All of that makes it a pleasure (and a worthwhile investment) to be a part of the experience of developing you. Your mentors and sponsors want to give of themselves to support you. The easier you can make it for them to engage the more beneficial the relationship will be.

As in every relationship, you'll want to be sensitive to the boundaries. There are people who will gladly give you an hour of their time, and others for whom it might be appropriate to take 10 minutes. You're the fortunate recipient of another's generosity and goodwill. Be sure you don't cross the line and take more than they are willing to give. When they have been supportive of you, be supportive of them—whether that means protecting their boundaries, being sensitive to their time, or looking for ways to ensure their investment in you is well spent.

Chemistry

The second condition to a successful relationship is chemistry.

In this case, we're interested in intellectual chemistry, which is not to be confused with personal chemistry. It doesn't matter whether you come from the same walks of life or share a history. It doesn't matter whether your lifestyles are the same or that you have similar home lives. It *does* matter that you have mutual respect.

You'll know you've found a good fit when you can talk and find valuable things to say that move your thinking forward and help accelerate your success. Your conversations create energy and ideas. You care about each other's success. You may agree or you may disagree, but there's enough equity in the relationship that you can debate and discuss the matters you need to get to a higher level. With the right chemistry, your relationships with your mentors and sponsors will be worthwhile.

Mutual Benefit

The third condition to embed in your mentoring and sponsoring experiences is mutual benefit. It doesn't have to be *equal* benefit. It's probably not going to be the *same* benefit, but there should be a reason for both of you to stay involved in the relationship.

Typically, your mentors and sponsors will be at a later stage in their career than you, and they likely will have achieved more than you have. That's why you're seeking their help. That doesn't mean working with you isn't also helpful for them. Think about what your mentors and sponsors get out of the situation.

- Is it a personal passion of theirs to develop other leaders?
- Are they excited about fostering the talent they see in you?

- Can you directly help them build their career and strengthen their reputation?
- Is their primary goal the improvement of the organization?
- Do they have a vision to which you can contribute?

Getting a sense of why your mentors and sponsors are investing in you will help you design a mutually beneficial relationship.

It's tempting when you're with the people supporting you to let it be all about you. After all, you're the one looking to learn. But if you're in the game for a predetermined benefit that only serves you, the relationship won't prosper. The best relationships benefit both of you.

Joelle

Aspiring women unknowingly limit their careers when they lack mentors and sponsors. With the right skills and strategies, you can take control and get connected with the powerful people who can support your career.

Finding a Mentor or Sponsor

Many executives love the idea of having a mentor or a sponsor but are stopped at the very first step. How do you start?

All you really need to do is ask.

Look around you—in the business, in the industry, and in other sectors—and ask, "Who do I admire? Who can help me? What could I learn?" Gather some names. Look for variety so your relationships are balanced in terms of gender, power, and influence, so you are accessing a varied but powerful set of perspectives. Then call them up.

A simple, gracious request is easy to make.

- Mention how you know the person. ("I read your article." "I heard you at a conference." "I work with your team.")
- Tell them why you're getting in touch. ("I have a question I'd like to ask you." "I'm trying to learn more about something, and I thought you might have an interesting perspective.")
- Ask for their support. ("Would you be willing to have a brief conversation?")

By making it part of your routine to reach out to people and elicit their support, you'll soon find the people who can not just answer a question or two but also eventually become a long-term supporter.

Not every effort in your outreach will work out. That's okay. You don't have to ask directly for someone's long-term commitment on day one ("Will you be my mentor? Will you be my sponsor?"). In fact, it's better not to be so direct. You earn this kind of support rather than ask for it. Focus instead on building strong relationships with people who are in a position to help you improve your skills and your career.

One of the executives with whom I've worked developed an effective approach. Lynelle was a senior manager in a management consulting firm with a long list of contacts but no strong supporters or advocates. When she realized she needed to strengthen these kinds of relationships, she and I pulled out of her network a short list of names: a diverse cross section of leaders who had the potential (and a reason) to invest extensively in her. She started at the top of her organization and worked her way down, across, and even out of the firm, until she developed a list of candidates. They included:

- The CEO.
- The head of Learning and Development.
- Her manager, his manager, and his manager's peers.
- Three women in various roles with an especially effective approach to leadership.
- The head of a recruiting firm who knew what organizations looked for in senior leaders.

Lynelle's list isn't a magic formula and may not match yours, but her process for identifying these leaders was effective. Once she had the names, she reached out. She sought them out at meetings, sat with them, and started conversations. She thought of meaningful questions to ask. She listened for opportunities to get involved in the projects of people she wanted to know. Behind the scenes, Lynelle kept track of her contacts and gave conscious thought to moving the relationships forward, but on a day-to-day basis, the process evolved naturally over time. Now Lynelle—who has recently been recognized for her leadership in the firm—is not just well *networked* but she's also *well known* as a star among the company leaders who want her to succeed.

You can take a similar approach. Decide who you want to talk to and just reach out. Soon you'll be surrounded by a team of supporters ready, willing, and able to support your success.

Maximizing the Opportunity

Once you have mentors and sponsors, make the most of the relationships. You may have to overcome some personal barriers to do this, especially if you're not accustomed to lobbying for yourself, but if you want to take advantage of the opportunity you've got to challenge yourself to ask for what you need—and follow through.

One of the strongest proponents I've met of mentoring and sponsorship is Camille Mirshokrai. Mirshokrai is the global director for Leadership Development at Accenture. She has developed practical tools and strategies for women on the specifics of how to find a mentor and a sponsor and how to make the relationships worthwhile on both sides. "To effectively solicit the help of an individual who will fight for us and help open doors for us, we must first be clear with ourselves about what we want," says Mirshokrai.

In addition, once we know what we want, we need to ask for what we need to get there. Mirshokrai pinpointed the reason why many women don't get the support they need: "Asking for sponsorship equals asking for help."

If you are someone who doesn't like to ask for help, you'll need to move past that. You will go further, learn more, and feel stronger when you realize success is a group effort. Adopt a new mindset: you are committed to making an impact, you're valuable, and you deserve the advantage of strong supporters. Don't be afraid to ask for help. It's a key that opens the door to a successful future.

Maintaining the Momentum

There are many ways to maintain relationships with your mentors and sponsors. Be prepared and use the time well, just as you would want someone else to do for you.

Nora Denzel, formerly an executive at Intuit and now an executive advisor and popular keynote speaker, has a formula for approaching your advocates that keeps the relationship moving forward. Every time you meet, bring two things:

1. A Demonstrate and
2. An Ask.

Imagine you've met with your sponsor. He's given you direction that you should expand your knowledge into other parts of the business. So you do. You invite yourself to a meeting or two outside your usual job responsibilities, and you start to understand how your goals connect to other initiatives throughout the company. You start collaborating with peers and generating new ideas for how you can work together toward mutual goals.

But don't stop there. Now is the time to go back to your sponsor with a Demonstrate and an Ask.

First, the Demonstrate. Take the time to share what you've learned. This isn't grandstanding ("Look what I did!"). You're contributing to a conversation about the business, while at the same time validating the time your sponsor spent with you and inviting further insight. This kind of conversation can deepen your learning. It shows you to be a leader. You're not bragging; you're participating. You have taken initiative. You are gaining expertise. By demonstrating how you've followed through, you show you're committed to the learning and worth their investment.

Next, the Ask. Keep the momentum going by knowing what you want to ask your sponsor next. I was reminded of this once when I facilitated a sponsoring conversation between a CEO and an up-and-coming leader in his company who wanted to know what she should be doing to advance her career. The woman asked her sponsor, "What do you think I should do?" Her sponsor replied, "You tell me. I need *you* to tell *me* what to do to help you be successful." If your sponsor posed the same question to you, how would you reply?

- Is there something you uncovered from your last meeting that your sponsor could help you understand?
- Is there something you'd like to try, do, or experience with which your sponsor could help?
- Is there something you need? Or some action you need your sponsor to take?

Take the lead in moving the relationship forward. One simple way to do this is to keep the pattern going every time, with a Demonstrate and an Ask.

Multiple Points on the Mountain

Think of your mentors and sponsors as your board of directors—the small subset of powerful people in your network who have direct influence on the growth of your career. One isn't enough. You need many.

An executive we interviewed—a president at an internationally known company—learned this lesson the hard way. "My career accelerated so quickly early on," she said. "I can't tell you that I recognized I had a sponsor. I didn't realize my boss was sponsoring me the way he did—but I knew it when he was gone. As soon as he left the company, my stock as a leader went down. It took years for me to build it back up."

For this very reason, Doreen Ida, who was recently promoted to president of Nestlé's Confections & Snacks Division, advises women to have "multiple points on the mountain."

> I liken it to mountain climbing. I would want as many attachments as possible to give me the support and confidence to keep pushing ahead. Having only one attachment to the mountain would actually be risky [in mountain climbing], and that is also true in the workplace.

As you build out your relationships, do your best to establish many different connections. Even the most secure of sponsorships is susceptible to change. People retire. People are fired. People move on. You'll be wise to secure a number of connections.

EXPERT ADVICE: DOES YOUR SPONSOR PASS THE TEST?

Sylvia Ann Hewlett, chairman and CEO of the Center for Talent Innovation (CTI) and the author of *Forget a Mentor, Find a Sponsor: The New Way to Fast-Track Your Career,* says that at a minimum, a sponsor must

- believe in you and go out on a limb for you,
- advocate for your next promotion, and
- provide air cover so you can take risks.

To qualify as a sponsor (not just a mentor), he or she must also do at least two of the following:

1. Expand your perception of what you can do.
2. Make connections for you to senior leaders.
3. Promote your visibility.
4. Open up career opportunities for you.
5. Offer advice on your style and performance.
6. Make connections for you outside the company.
7. Give advice.

In CTI research, when a diverse group including women and men were asked whether they believe they have a sponsor, 40 percent said yes. When this same group was prompted to measure their sponsor(s) against these criteria, the number slumped to 13 percent for women and 8 percent of non-Caucasians. As Hewlett summarizes the research, "few women and professionals of color differentiate between supporters and true sponsors." Women we have interviewed point out that many sponsors don't differentiate, either, thinking they are sponsoring women when they are merely mentoring—a special but not as productive skill.

How do your mentors and sponsors measure up?

Q&A with Howard and Joelle

I've heard some organizations try to organize mentoring and sponsorship into formal programs. What do you think of this approach?

Joelle: Well, I appreciate the effort on the part of the organizers to provide this structured support. Clearly there's a need. If mentoring and sponsorship are important to a woman's success, but many don't have a mentor or sponsor, then the efforts on the part of the organization do help. These programs can teach sponsors and protégés how to make the most of these relationships. They're not left to their own devices to pick up the phone and hope for the best. The programs provide tools. They outline expectations. Guidelines for making them successful. That could be helpful.

It's just that when I compare these manufactured affiliations to the more genuine relationships some leaders have, I can't help but think something's missing.

Howard: Unfortunately, even if they're well-intentioned, these programs can be another way of avoiding the elephant in the room—namely, that there may not be integrity in the selection process, the promotion process, and the treatment of women in the organization, such that they have to have a sponsor to argue on their behalf. If women aren't being promoted because the organization fundamentally doesn't embrace an ethic of diversity, a mentorship or sponsorship program can send the message that at least they're making an effort, even if it doesn't change the culture or the results.

Joelle: It seems a little cynical, but I can see your point. The assumption is that with mentoring and sponsorship, more women will be prepared and promoted, but if the organizational norms don't support that, then no amount of guidance will make it change.

Howard: In those cases, the programs can pacify people rather than grow them. Many of the programs I have seen over the last ten or fifteen years have dissolved, and for all the reasons we've talked about. People make the mistake of entering a program thinking their mentor or sponsor is going to handle their advancement, and they focus on that more than they focus on the learning.

Joelle: I also wonder how effective the relationship will be if it's foisted upon someone whether or not it's a good fit. Your mentor is supposed to devote a lot of time to you. What if they're not all that helpful? Your sponsor is supposed to fight for you, but what if they hardly even know you? The best programs match people well and take steps to support the development of a quality relationship.

Something about it still smacks of having to go to prom with the guy your dad picked out. I'm not sure the connection will really "take."

Howard: Perhaps the best role for these programs to play is to make the introduction. You still need take responsibility for the success of the relationship and the outcomes.

Should my boss be my mentor or sponsor?

Howard: Why should sponsorship be separated from good leadership? Your boss should definitely be doing this. Whether or not you have other mentors and sponsors, a good leader will be committed to developing you.

Joelle: What if you don't like your boss?

Howard: I think you have to ask yourself, how many people got promoted when their sponsor believed in them but their boss did not? That percentage would be so low. Mentoring and sponsorships are very effective techniques, but you have to be careful it doesn't become a fantasy. Just because you have a mentor or a sponsor doesn't mean you're a shoe-in for the job you want. If you don't like your boss, the solution isn't to run to your mentor or sponsor. What you should be doing is improving your relationship with your boss.

Joelle: What advice do you have for how to do that well?

Howard: First, wherever possible don't put your boss in a situation which lowers candor. In other words, you don't want to create a relationship in which your boss doesn't want to give you candid feedback. You don't want a relationship in which you cause problems or challenges for your boss. Foster an open relationship based on trust, just as you would with a friend or a spouse. Otherwise, your boss is just going to tell you what you want to hear, because it's the path of least resistance.

Now, that may require patience. If you're going to build a relationship with your boss, you may have to put up with the stupid things that leave his lips. If your boss is a little rough around the edges, if he or she is not always the most sensitive person in the room, or if he or she says some things you don't agree with, well, take it in context. Are these deal breakers? Be careful you don't judge a few little things too harshly if on balance your boss means more good than harm. If you do find yourself in a situation where you and your boss are at odds, consider a fresh start. Offer to begin again on the right foot and develop the relationship from scratch, building trust along the way.

Joelle: It's an important relationship. The best bosses I've seen believe that part of their job as leaders is to mentor their employees, sponsor them, make sure they're successful, teach them what they need to learn, celebrate their results, and defend them to make sure they get the best opportunities. They are manager, mentor and sponsor all in one. That, to me, seems like a smart way to build an organization.

Melissa: The End of the Story

There was a time Melissa struggled with insecurity about her leadership. If she wasn't careful, self-doubt could turn into anxiety and then fear. Before she knew it, she was wrestling with the idea that maybe she wasn't very significant at work and wondering whether it was worth it to keep going.

It was only through a leadership development program for high-performing leaders that she realized what she had been missing all along: sponsorship. Even though she'd had beloved mentors throughout her life, she had never had a powerful advocate backing her career and moving it forward.

Melissa's organization was just implementing a formal sponsorship program, so she got on board. She sought out the head of Talent Development to talk it over. Who in the organization was a natural connector? Who had enough seniority and clout to help her forge a career path? Who would be open to advocating for her when decisions were being made about promotions or other career-advancing opportunities? The head of Talent Development promised to give it some thought.

A few days later, armed with a few good names and a little bit of pluck, Melissa started placing phone calls. She arranged a series of conversations with people she wanted to get to know—and whom Melissa wanted to know her. She crafted a few thoughtful questions about the business and set out to learn two things. First, she wanted to get the answers to her questions. Second, she was looking for a mutually beneficial opportunity, a sense of chemistry, and potential for real results.

From there, the process took on a life of its own.

Within months of starting her search for a sponsor, Melissa could be found sitting regularly at the table in the corner café with one of the chief officers of her company, talking animatedly about the challenges of the business and looking to involve Melissa as a talented member of the team. Eventually, her sponsor introduced her to a number of opportunities to develop her expertise and prepare her to take on bigger responsibilities. No longer afraid of the power in the boardroom—or her own power— Melissa finally had the advantage she'd been hoping for.

Key Points

1. Mentoring is taking an interest *in* you. Sponsorship is taking action *for* you.
2. Even women who do have a healthy network can end up over-mentored and under-sponsored.
3. When leaders have strong mentors and sponsors in place, they feel supported and championed.
4. Only 13 percent of full-time female employees at large companies have sponsors or colleagues senior enough to make a career-changing impact with their support, compared to 46 percent of men.[9]
5. Women in leadership must educate themselves about the benefits of mentors and sponsors, fill those roles, and cultivate and leverage the relationships.

Questions for Reflection

1. Have you ever had a truly beneficial relationship? What made it so? How could you create that again?
2. Who are the three people you most admire in your professional circle—the ones who help you learn, excel, and advance?
3. Who do you connect with naturally? How are you involving them in your career?
4. Think through the relationships you'd like to develop. If you need a mentor, why? What would you gain? If you're looking for a sponsor, why? What are you hoping will happen?
5. What is your immediate next step?

CHAPTER 4

The Executive Presence Advantage (How do you know you're perceived as a leader?)

"Presence is more than just looking the part of an executive. It is looking it, feeling it, acting it, and believing it."
—Kim Hanna, Global Environmental Officer, AIG

Brooke

Brooke was a high-performing senior vice president for a Fortune 500 telecommunications company. She got glowing performance reviews and her colleagues and direct reports all respected her.

One day her boss pulled the chief HR officer into his office. "I know Brooke is starting to think about her next promotion," he confided, "and I'd like her to be considered for my role. Confidentially, I'm moving on into a new position in the company, and I see her as a natural fit. The problem is none of the other guys do. We were in a meeting yesterday talking about my successor and her name never even came up!"

The chief HR officer was stunned—and concerned. "She didn't even come up? But she's a natural candidate for the job."

"I know," said Brooke's boss. "I think so, too. But there's no way she's going to get it. It's not that she couldn't do the job. It's just that no one else sees her in that role."

On paper, Brooke looked like the ideal successor. What was missing that kept her from a promotion? Why would a star performer not even be considered for a position being vacated by her boss? It wasn't that she couldn't do the job. She wasn't even being *noticed*. She was completely overlooked. Brooke was well liked and well prepared. But in this case, she was also invisible. In their minds, she simply didn't fit the part.

What Brooke didn't know was what she was missing: executive presence.

Executive presence is a vital sign of your readiness to take on bigger leadership roles.[1] Yet, many leaders don't know what executive presence actually *is*, much less if they have it. That would be worrisome, except for the fact that you can change it.

You can shape your presence to project an image consistent with who you want to be and the opportunities you want to have. In this chapter, we show you how to develop presence intentionally—transforming yourself into the vision of a compelling leader.

The Executive Presence Dilemma

Executive presence is the degree to which others perceive you to be a leader.

The trap leaders sometimes fall into is being underestimated by others because of the way they present themselves. They may be perfectly capable, but if their presence doesn't project the expected image of a leader, they may be seen as less powerful than they are.

Some of the leaders we've coached illustrate his point.

- Lucy was a shy, quiet woman—a strong performer and a respected leader to her company. Despite a large team and considerable influence, she seemed to almost disappear into the walls in most meetings, where no one seemed to seek her opinion.
- Flora was vivacious—more cheerleader than senior manager in most settings. Her warmth and enthusiasm made her a favorite among employees, and her managers loved her for the kind, compassionate tone she brought to their teams. But for higher-level meetings and more serious business discussions, with her light-hearted style, it was evident the more senior executives didn't take her seriously.
- Joanie was a paradox: a diminutive powerhouse. She was small in stature, young for her role, and 20 years the junior of the partners in her law firm. She had an Ivy League education, an illustrious client list, and a winning track record, but in the huge conference rooms filled with authoritative, commanding lawyers, she was often dismissed.

All of these women brought more to their roles than met the eye. They could sense they weren't perceived as powerful, and they saw the signs— being interrupted by others, having others take over their ideas, not being approached for their professional opinions even in their areas of expertise. But they didn't know why. Being undervalued in this way was unnerving.

What these women needed was executive presence. That may sound like a simple enough solution, but acquiring presence can be complicated for women. Women get mixed messages about what counts as executive presence, if they get those messages at all. Presence can be a sensitive topic, and they may not get the feedback they need to get it right.

Femininity—The Double Bind

The first hurdle women face when tackling executive presence is the fear that for others to view them as leaders, they'll have to stop being themselves.

They're not imagining it. With historically few women holding high-level leadership positions, the image of what executive presence should be is often based on a man.

> One of the more entrenched and limiting beliefs is that there are certain styles, approaches, or behaviors required to be a successful leader . . . [W]ith hiring managers at senior levels being predominantly male, the often assumed "appropriate and necessary" leadership approaches would be those similar to their own. The result: women are unfairly deemed to have the wrong leadership style needed to be successful.[2]

Until they resolve these contradictions, businesswomen are trapped in a quandary—"caught . . . in the double bind of combining being an ideal manager, which means being masculine, with being an ideal woman, which means being feminine."[3]

You will be most successful developing executive presence when you're able to present yourself as a leader while still maintaining your natural strengths and style. That requires a sense of self, as well as a clear understanding of others' expectations. That brings us to the second hurdle.

Feedback—The Third Rail

The second hurdle women face when tackling executive presence is the sensitivity of the topic.

There are many reasons executive presence is difficult to discuss. The details of presence can be personal, and people can be hesitant to point them out. They know feedback on flaws is painful and they may be afraid to insult you or hurt your feelings. On both the giving and the receiving end, it's just not easy to approach the topic.

Women, in particular, have trouble getting feedback on their presence—especially when it comes to appearance. One article calls this the "third rail" in feedback, and many men don't want to touch it. Beyond being embarrassing, sometimes the truth isn't even advisable. How can a male boss tell his female peer her neckline is too low? How can a female executive tell a direct report her style is outdated? As true as those opinions may be, they can get the one providing feedback into hot water. In one instance, the European bank tried to put out a manual to help women improve their presence ("wear a conservative nail polish color, and choose neutral lingerie"). It was so skewered in the press that they withdrew the manual altogether. In other words, women must have executive presence in their appearance and bearing, but information about what presence should be is often lacking, and if they get it wrong, no one will tell them.

Appearance is only one small element of presence, but apparently it's an important one. Specific details of appearance, like unkempt attire and provocative clothing, can undercut presence by up to 75 percent.[4] Complicating the issue is the fact that it's so difficult to address. According to research from the Center for Talent Innovation, "Women are much more highly scrutinized for how they look and dress than their male peers but are 32 percent less likely . . . to get any feedback from male superiors."[5]

These are precisely the reasons the term "executive presence" is so essential. The concept of presence conveys that there are certain expectations, mannerisms, and stylistic indicators that communicate, "I have what it takes, and I'm ready to fill the role of a leader."

Resolving this dilemma is a more than a matter of managing perception. It's also about being confident in yourself. The more you can learn about the impressions you make on others, the more you can shape your image to fit their expectations. At the same time, you can work on strengthening your self-image.

It's tempting at this point to provide a laundry list of where women go wrong with executive presence and how to get it right. Indeed, many books on women in leadership do just this, and certainly having concrete examples of what works and what doesn't can be helpful.

It can also derail you.

First of all, the feedback women get on their presence is often colored by personal preference. It can be hard to distinguish when presence is an issue you need to correct versus bias in the eye of the beholder.

Second, to imply that presence is an issue more for women than for men would be misleading. Men struggle with presence, too.

Third, trying to describe a one-size-fits-all model of presence would deny the variety that makes us all who we are. Giving too much credence to whether or not you have executive presence can make you self-conscious of your every move. We'd like to avoid that.

Instead, we prefer to focus on solutions and provide a way of understanding presence that will help you choose for yourself how you want to be perceived.

The Executive Presence Advantage

When you have the advantage of executive presence, your intent matches your impact. You become more visible. You're seen as an equal. As a result, you develop a reputation as a leader, and that leads to more and better opportunities.

Kristi Hedges, the author of *The Power of Presence: Unlock Your Potential to Influence and Engage Others,* describes presence this way:

> [Presence is] equal parts communication aptitude, mental attitude, and authentic style. It combines a supportive inner mindset with the outer skills needed to create the natural, confident, consistent leadership presence we all seek.[6]

In order to master executive presence, you'll need a proper sense of what your presence should be. It's important to get a clear definition of executive presence and measure yourself against it, so you can be sure you're having the impact on others that you want.

Executive Presence: A Dimension of Leadership

Executive presence manifests in the silent judgments people make about you, rightly or wrongly. The more specifics you can get about how you're being measured, the better you can assess yourself.

A review of the research on executive presence revealed an expansive list of attributes:

- **Status and Reputation:** the roles you've held, an impressive network, and significant accomplishments.
- **Physical Characteristics:** your grooming, dress, stature, and mannerisms.
- **Demeanor:** your confidence and composure.

- **Communication Skills:** the degree to which you are compelling and articulate.
- **Interpersonal Skills:** your ability to connect with others easily.
- **Interpersonal Behavior Patterns:** your warmth and genuine connections, irrespective of rank or role.
- **Values-in-Action:** your integrity, authenticity, and trustworthiness.
- **Intellect and Expertise:** the knowledge you have gained from your education and experience.
- **Work Outcomes:** your energy, sense of responsibility, and ability to achieve results.
- **Power Use:** the degree to which you are commanding and exercise authority.

Using your ability to read others' reactions, you can shape your presence intentionally, to make a positive impact. Along with your intelligence, experience, and performance, presence is another dimension that shows other people you're a leader.

There's one more element of presence that's essential to being successful:

- **A Sense of Self.** Executive presence shows up to others as the outward expression of your leadership but originates from within.

In part, you will find your sense of self by integrating your personal style with the expectations of executive presence. Doing this well turns out to be one of the fortunate advantages for women in leadership, points out Larissa Herda, president and CEO of Time Warner.

> Being firm, fair, consistent and decisive (traditionally masculine traits) is not contradictory to being compassionate and caring (traditionally feminine traits). If you bring those things together as an executive, you get the hearts and minds of your people.

When you find your unique way of expressing executive presence, you will naturally develop a stronger sense of yourself as a leader. You'll feel powerful, and it will show.

The Benefits of Executive Presence

In a survey of executives, *Forbes* magazine found "executive presence" counts for 26 percent of what it takes to get promoted.[7]

When you have strong presence:

- You gain a certain level of respect.
- Your presence engenders trust among others, causing them to listen to you and take you seriously.
- Your credibility leads to concrete results. People want to promote you, do business with you, give you better assignments, and recommend you to others.

Improving your presence will enhance your image and leave you feeling—and viewed by others—as a leader.

Our Perspectives

Howard

This is a topic I've come to know a lot about. Throughout my career, I've been the one who's had to have the conversation with the man with the unbearable breath or the woman leaning over the copier exposing all. From both sides of the table, it can be an awkward conversation, but a careful approach to addressing the situation can definitely help.

It's important, too, because when it comes to presence, awareness is everything. You can't change what you don't know. Somehow we have to learn to communicate.

The Wrong Way: Digs and Barbs

Men (and let's face it—women, too) aren't always good at giving feedback, especially when it's awkward. Often what men do is to try humor to get their message across. They use sarcasm or make little digs. It's hurtful. It stings, especially because it strikes at the core of who a person is. When someone's boss takes a crack at them, it can affect the relationship in the exact opposite way that's intended: turning people off, offending them, and causing a rift and resentment. The person walks away feeling angry and judged.

It may actually be helpful to realize that when a comment is unfavorable, people tend to come at it indirectly. Listen to people when they joke and jab. See if there's any truth to what they say. If they give you a light-hearted feedback, dig a little deeper to see what prompted their remark. If the time isn't right, circle back to them later and follow up ("You said something earlier I wanted to follow up on . . ."). Be sure to make it safe, and they'll be more likely to open up and make a comment you can actually use.

The Right Way: A Matter of Respect

Imagine you want feedback on your presence. What do you say?

Here's a scenario. There was a man in one of the firms I worked for who was poorly groomed. To put it candidly, he had body odor and unbearable breath. People had worked with him for a couple of years and apparently had never addressed the issue. I decided, it's time to talk to him. It is impacting the customer. There was no question the customer was uneasy. I said, "It's awkward for me to talk about this with you, but it's something I think is important, because it affects your credibility, especially in our business. I can't speak for anywhere else, but in our business this is important. Can I be honest with you?" He said yes, and I told him. I gave it to him straight. "You smell and you have bad breath. Let's talk about how I can help." The guy came up and hugged me. He said, "My best friends have never told me this." He was able to make a change in some areas that were embarrassing to talk about—but not nearly as embarrassing as walking around thinking he was fine when everyone else is crossing the room when they saw him coming.

Now think of how badly that conversation would have gone if I had used sarcasm to try to tell this man the same thing. He wouldn't have believed me; he'd just feel insulted.

Executive presence can be sensitive. People who address it poorly end up doing more harm than good. It's so much better to communicate with respect.

What if you're on the other end of the conversation? How can you *get* feedback that is respectful, if you really want to check on the impression you make? You can take control of the conversation and ask for the clear feedback. It might sound something like this:

"I want to make sure I'm making a good impression. I want to be sure if there's something I do or something about how I present myself that's a little off or that could be improved, that I know what it is. I want to be sure there isn't a way I portray myself that's working against me. I know if I ask most people, I'm not going to get a straight answer. Can you do me a favor and let me know if there is? I'd appreciate you telling me, and if you don't see anything, could you keep your ears open and let me know?"

Address matters of presence with a sense of respect—respect for others and respect for yourself. Your ability to ask for feedback and to make it okay for people to give it honestly will get you the information you need.

Your Way: A Matter of Choice

You may feel defensive when you get feedback on presence. It might help to objectify the topic for a moment and realize it's not just in the corporate office that presence matters. It's everywhere. Police officers need to be commanding, confident, and calm. Newscasters need to appear friendly and informed. Counselors need to be warm and unassuming. And leaders need to inspire trust and confidence. The way people experience you must fit the expectations for the role.

It's also a matter of choice. It's not that different than the other choices you make professionally. Sometimes it's a matter of education: if you want to be a doctor, you have to get a medical degree. If you don't want to put in the work to get a medical degree, then don't choose to be a doctor—but don't blame other people for not giving you the opportunity to be a doctor. Now apply that logic to presence: if you want to be a CEO, you have to be and act and look like a CEO. If you don't want to be and act and look like a CEO, then don't have the dream of being a CEO. It's about aligning to the expectations of the role.

Joelle

In my work with executive women, perhaps no single term has been as helpful as *executive presence*. Before we had a name for this aspect of leadership, talented leaders were unknowingly and perhaps unconsciously being rejected with no way to understand why.

Now we have better language to define the subtle qualities of well-regarded leaders. However, executive presence is still an elusive topic and not one easily discussed. In this section, I'll share the experience of one of my clients, along a few of the lessons she learned that you can learn, too. We'll end with a few suggestions for anyone wanting to be seen as a strong and self-assured leader.

"Before and After:" An Image of Executive Presence

Laura Gibb was the CFO of a retail company. When I first met Laura, she was an executive who was competent, but reserved. She had worked in the company for 25 years, and her experience gave her great credibility. But despite a substantial résumé and a supportive team, there was something about Laura that made her seem somewhat less powerful than she really was.

As Laura's executive coach, I had the privilege of interviewing a number of her colleagues, and they helped us discover what it was. Despite universal positive feedback from her team, Laura's managers saw her as missing a certain something. A bit of strength perhaps. A sense of self. *Presence.*

The word on the street was that Laura was a competent leader, but she seemed to be hiding in the shadows.

Fast-forward a year and a half. The last day of our coaching engagement, I walked into Laura's office, in her top floor executive office. In front of the windows overlooking a stunning view of the San Francisco bay, a woman stood tall and relaxed. She was smiling. She had style. She looked *strong.* Laura may not have known exactly what "presence" meant when she heard it first, but she certainly had it now. Once a woman sitting quietly behind a desk, here stood an executive clearly leading, out in front.

Making the Shift

What did Laura discover in her journey to understand executive presence? What made the difference?

Executives like Laura who consciously shift into a strong sense of presence tend to go through a series of phases.

Awareness. At some point in their careers, people sometimes experience a dawning awareness that they are seen as "less than" a leader. The realization becomes clarified as they look around at whose careers are taking off and whose are not, and they may start to compare themselves to others. Or, they may get direct or indirect critiques on their appearance, approach, or reputation that tells them they don't have the respect they need to attain that next level of leadership. Becoming aware of the perception others have of you and being willing to consider their opinion is an important (and brave) first step.

Laura's biggest shift was an awareness of her own importance. She had to learn, by processing her feedback and really listening to it, that she had a reputation for excellence. She had to believe it herself, as much as her boss and her sponsor believed in her. She had to recognize that her title meant something. It meant she knew what she was talking about. It meant other people trusted her judgment. They wanted her to speak up, to have vision, and to *lead.*

Acceptance. In addition to becoming aware of their impact on others, leaders I've met who have broached the topic of presence have to bring themselves to take the matter seriously.

Several executives I've worked with who have received feedback on their presence have had an initially negative reaction. The elements of presence are largely subjective, and comments about presence poorly expressed can come across as judgmental or degrading. In instances that truly cross the line, feedback bleeds into prejudice.

You may have a tendency to dismiss feedback when you find it offensive or unfair. Many an executive woman has said to me, "If my manager thinks I'm too this or not enough that, that's *his* problem." Well, yes, except that his problem has a direct impact on your career.

Laura herself had to sift through the feedback and determine what to accept and what to reject. In doing so, she seemed to strengthen her sense of self-worth. She didn't have to accept feedback she couldn't endorse and some of it to her seemed frankly inappropriate. But she did find other information she could use.

Education. Once people move past the initial stages in which they become aware of the importance of executive presence and accept that it's a real aspect of leadership, then they turn the corner and start to learn. In many cases, opening the door to discovery about executive presence is a game changer. Suddenly it becomes apparent that there's much to learn and change, most of it under your control.

- You can experiment with various communication styles to create an effect—from storytelling to platform speaking to effective use of silence.
- You can develop a more advanced awareness of how to interact in any setting, from conflict to a developmental discussion to a heated debate—all while maintaining your composure and having a positive impact.
- You can manage your reputation—staying wide open to any indicators that show you're having the effect on others you want to make.
- You can learn to read people and predict—even influence—their responses.
- You can make changes in your appearance so that others take you seriously, find you approachable, or any other impression you might be trying to create.

Developing executive presence can be as simple as modifying an attitude here or a bad habit there, but it can also be a stage of great transformation— one in which you finally see yourself as a leader and make sure everyone else sees you that way, too. You will act differently because you feel different. Everyone else will sense it, too.

Lessons in Developing Presence

In addition to the longer-term changes in perspective we've discussed so far, there are a few other shortcuts that can get you started.

Look the part. I've heard executive presence misinterpreted as "style." Presence more than just wearing a fancy suit. But you *do* need to look the part. As a leader, you are playing a role. You are a leader in the company. You are seen by others as actually representing that company. Do you see yourself that way, too, and if you do, then how should you (literally) appear? One suggestion is to dress as you would for the role you want to have. It may not be politically correct to say it, but it's true: appearance matters.

Pay attention to your self-talk. Give yourself a mantra. If it helps, get your coach, manager, mentor, sponsor, or colleague to reflect back to you how you are at your best. Tell yourself you're powerful. Don't let the doubtful voices in the back of your mind hold you back. You are valuable, you are important, you matter.

Sit up front. One of the things women learn to observe about themselves is that in the conference room they too often take a seat in the back. The *way* back. Away from the table. The next time you're in a conference room, watch who sits where. Where are the people who have power? Where are the people who have presence? Who's hiding in the back? Take a deep breath, stand tall, and choose a seat up front. You deserve a seat at the table. You wouldn't have been invited to be there otherwise.

Say it out loud. Not only are you invited to sit at the table in whatever meetings you attend, *you are also expected to participate.* Too many women sit back and let everyone else do the talking. Why? Is it out of courtesy? Kindness? Deference? Lack of confidence? Maybe none of these apply; maybe you're just quiet. It's okay if you don't believe you need to say something just to hear yourself talk. The point isn't to fill airspace or hog the limelight. Just consider that you are present in any setting because you have something valuable to add. You have opinions, expertise, and experience that will help shape the dialogue. Say it out loud!

Associate with power. In order for you to truly have power, you do have to be authentic and you don't have to be someone you aren't. On the other hand, you do likely have relationships with powerful people. Is that a secret? Once again, out of respect or (ironically) self-confidence, women don't always find it preferable to stand out in the crowd or take center stage. One way to increase your sense of self as an influential, deserving leader is to be a part of that crowd—sitting with them, spending time with them, seeing yourself as one of them, and choosing them as your peers. (Because they are.)

Executive presence is an essential element of success in corporate life. From your shoes to your soul, you can show yourself to be a competent, confident leader who deserves a seat at the table.

AN ALTERNATIVE PERSPECTIVE

It's important when discussing presence to consider the two sides of this topic. Some say it's important to know the rules of the business environment, and how else can women know the rules when they were originally written by men? Others are intuitively offended by this notion that there's one ideal way to be a leader and feel strongly it's the culture that should change, not the way women express themselves at work.

One executive who feels this way is Stormy Simon, copresident of Overstock.com. Here's how she described to us her view of executive presence.

"I think as women we need to embrace who we are. The actor Morgan Freeman once said, "I don't want a Black History Month. Black history is American history." Well, I don't want lessons in executive presence. My presence as a woman should be just as valid in a corporate setting as a man's.

"We do things differently. I'm not going to cut my hair. I'm not going to dress like a man. I'm going to wear make-up and love it. I'm going to wear cute things. I'm not going to give that up. I love my femininity. I love it at work, and I love it at home. If I want to cry, I will. If something makes me emotional and brings me to tears, I don't think that makes me weak. It's like laughing—it's an emotional response! I'm okay with being passionate and sensitive and all the beautiful things women are. Does that mean I'm a weaker president . . . or a stronger one? Does it make me a weaker board member . . . or a stronger one?"

The world is changing, and that includes the corporate world. In the meantime, as an executive and a woman, your best bet is to understand fully what it will take to be the *you* you want to be.

Q&A with Howard and Joelle

Your remark about sarcasm and humor seems true to me. Men do seem to communicate that way, but I don't know that it's always clear whether they're being honest or just joking. How can I tell?

Joelle: Men will use humor with each other to communicate difficult messages, and I suppose if it's part of their culture, the message gets through. It must come as a surprise for them when it backfires so badly with women.

The downside to this communication breakdown is the missed opportunity. I've seen women react so badly to that kind of remark that it ruins the relationship. I've also seen them take a comment so seriously that it crushes their ambitions. They can be so offended they turn completely off. These are reactions the person making the comment could have never imagined and almost certainly didn't intend. But through all the noise created by this emotional reaction, there's actually a fairly simple, valid, well-intentioned (if badly communicated) message. If you can train yourself not to take things too personally, there could be a lot to learn. You might not like hearing that you come across as timid or that your presentation lacks finesse, but those may be symptoms of a deeper issue—like confidence or composure—that you want to address.

Howard: These situations are delicate. Where many people go wrong is they judge or they tell people how they should be or how they should change. When I give feedback on presence, it's not my job to make a decision for them. I'm just laying out the facts.

You talk about executive presence as if it's a choice, but what about those characteristics people can't change?

Joelle: It seems to me there are some areas people can't change, or feel they can't change. You can argue that people always have a choice, and theoretically that may be true, but in practical terms they may not feel that they do. What if they just have a subtler style? Or the opposite—what if their style is naturally brusque? What if, for any reason, their intent doesn't match their impact, and they don't feel they can change?

Howard: One way to handle that is to be transparent. Do it privately if you prefer, and perhaps only with people you trust, but share what's going on with you. "Just so you know, I tend to be this way, and here's the effect it may have. I wanted you to know so it doesn't come across in a negative way. I just want to make sure I'm having a positive impact." From personality and style, to personal mannerisms and characteristics, to particulars of your appearance, and even medical conditions, this approach can give you a safe way to express yourself and avoid being misread.

You get to decide whether you want to be open about these things or keep them private. You don't have to say anything to anyone. What you can't do is keep everything private but expect everyone else to somehow know.

If you can change and you don't, you have to accept responsibility for that. If you can't change or find it difficult to change, you can also accept responsibility for that. You have to learn to govern yourself.

I've always believed my work should speak for itself, and that seems to pay off. Does executive presence really matter?

Joelle: In all the heart-to-hearts I've had with women over presence, there always comes a point where they ask this question. Does it really matter? It's draining trying to be all things to all people. There can be almost a helplessness at that moment—a feeling that, "I am who I am, and if that's not good enough, is this a place I really want to work?" We all have to sort through that question. Each of us has to decide for ourselves. What she's searching for is, do I want to conform in this way, when what I really want is to be valued for who I am?

Howard: It's a fair question. Here's what I can tell you: no one has ever been fired for a lack of presence. At least, it's far more likely to go the other way, meaning people will choose to leave when they sense there's not a fit between who they are and where they work.

The big question at the heart of the matter is, what do the job and the customer require?

If the job and the customer require a certain look and feel on your part, then presence matters. If your presence or lack of presence affects the way people see you, how they respond to you, whether they respect you, and so on, you need to be aware and choose your presentation for the response you want.

If you don't want to change, that's your choice. Just know the consequences. If you're okay with the consequences, don't change. If not, then do change. It's always up to you.

In addition to the big question ("Is it affecting the business or the customer?") here are a few more versions you can ask yourself to decide where presence really matters:

- Is it mandatory?
- Is it important for your career growth and advancement?
- Is it keeping people from taking you seriously?

Joelle: They're all good questions. It's so much harder to change when you don't want to or don't feel you should have to. Considering these questions can get to a more genuine, less defensive answer, and one you can live with. If you think your brazen attitude or your soft-spoken style is a charming part of your style, you might choose to embrace it and forget about everyone else. Or, if you're trying to fit into a culture that prefers a different style than yours, you might work on expanding the range of how you act and interact.

Howard: I'm not sure people have the right to ask an organization to change to be flexible to them. The norms and expectations are what they are. It's up to you to decide if you want to live with them.

Brooke: The End of the Story

Brooke sat down with the chief HR officer of her company to talk about the promotion she had been hoping to get. When she learned she hadn't gotten the job, she was crushed. When she heard the reason, she was confused.

"Don't see me in that role?" she asked. "How can they not see me in that role? I have every qualification!" Ever the fighter, Brooke wanted to know exactly what she could do to increase her chances of getting the job the next time. What could she do to improve?

Here the chief HR officer had few answers. "You are qualified. I don't think this is about your performance or results. What you really need now is executive presence. The other executives like you and know you, but they don't necessarily see you as a leader. If you're going to step up to their level, they're going to have to see you as one of them."

The chief HR officer offered to work with Brooke to develop executive presence. Brooke took on the challenge.

1. *She got a 360-degree profile—not just data, but a detailed, specific, descriptive report from her bosses, peers, and direct reports to understand how she came across and the impact it had on others.*
2. *She got coaching on her presence from people she trusted to give her honest feedback.*
3. *She took the advice and she also started watching and being mindful of how others who were seen as strong leaders conducted themselves.*
4. *She developed criteria and started measuring herself against it, occasionally checking her self-perception with others.*

As a result, she could sense herself becoming elevated in the eyes of her colleagues. Although she couldn't put her finger on what was different, she could tell they were taking her more seriously. She'd always known she was a leader. Now everyone else knew it, too.

Key Points

1. Executive presence is the degree to which others perceive you to be a leader.
2. The trap leaders sometimes fall into is being underestimated by others because of the way they present themselves. They may be perfectly capable, but if their presence doesn't project the expected image of a leader, they may be seen as less powerful than they are.
3. Women get mixed messages about what counts as executive presence, if they get those messages at all. Presence can be a sensitive topic, and they may not get the feedback they need to get it right.
4. When you have executive presence, your intent matches your impact.
5. Resolving this dilemma is a more than a matter of managing perception. It's also about being confident in yourself.

Questions for Reflection

1. What is the impression you want to make?
2. Is that the impression you do make? How do you know?
3. How could you find out how others perceive you as a leader?
4. Who can help you honestly tailor your approach to make the best impact?
5. Are there things you feel challenged by when it comes to executive presence—that you either disagree with or feel you can't address? What can you do to resolve them?

CHAPTER 5

The Performance Advantage (How do you outperform your highest expectations?)

"At the end of the day, it's not about being a woman or a man. The first thing you have to do is deliver."

—Annette Thompson, Senior Vice President and Chief Learning Officer, Farmers Insurance

Cynthia

Cynthia sat back in her chair in exasperation. The president of a property in a prestigious brand of hotels and resorts, she had clearly reached the end of her rope.

"I don't know what else to do," she said, turning up her hands. "What else can I do? I have the highest performing property in the company. By every measure we are the best. I generate the highest revenue. We have the best customer satisfaction. Our employees are the most highly engaged. I've been clear about my desire to move to a corporate position and I've gotten all the feedback I can think of. It's all positive. Yet there's no attention to my performance. When I ask the CEO to tell me what more I can do to advance my career, he has nothing to say. And yet, here I am. Just the manager of a property. The proud manager, but a manager just the same. I give up. It's clear this is where I'll stay."

With consistently great results on her performance measures, Cynthia didn't know what else to say about her results. There was nothing else to do but keep achieving as she had always done. All she could do was try to find peace within herself.

Cynthia belonged to a mastermind group of other executive women. With their coaching and counsel, she made her decision. "I know I'm not going to get recognized. I'm not giving up on myself, I'm just facing reality. I love what I do and I'll keep doing it."

And she did. Cynthia remained a highly regarded president of her property year after year.

Occasionally she got frustrated again and started to question her decision.

"Should I jump ship?" she considered. "Go somewhere where there's more mobility and a merit-based culture? Should I leave corporate life and go into consulting? Should I retire?" Her intuition told her no, no, and no. "I have to stop spinning and remember this is my choice. I love what I do, I love this company, and this is where I want to work. Do I wish things were different? Yes, I do, but at the same time, I'm willing to accept what I can't change."

Cynthia continued to excel. She made sure to share her results and took credit where credit was due. Then she turned her attention squarely to her work and immersed herself in being the best property president she could be—happy most days, with the occasional fleeting feeling of regret.

In the leadership layer just below the executive committee, women like Cynthia abound. They are proud of their results and have the records to back them up, but they can't for the life of them figure out why their good work goes undiscovered.

Make your performance count. You can make great strides by understanding the advantages of exceptional performance. Throughout the ups and downs of a career, it may be the best thing you can do for yourself. In this chapter, we talk about how you can not just achieve great performance but also how to turn your results into a rewarding career.

The Performance Dilemma

Performance is the degree to which you do your job well. Using whatever outcomes matter most in your organization and your role, your performance is measured by your results.

Leaders want their results to count. They want to know their efforts will make a positive impact on their careers, whether that means building their reputation, getting new opportunities, or being rewarded for their good work. Unfortunately, there's no guarantee. Corporate life is more complex than that.

One of our clients learned this painful lesson the hard way.

Renee was the head of a large division of a major lending institution who had for many years been credited for pulling her division through the recession safely. She had poured every ounce of her work effort into turning things around and was incredibly successful, but in so doing neglected to develop herself in other ways—for instance, by maintaining relationships with key leaders of the organization or thinking strategically about whether she was being perceived as a leader. She trusted her good work to speak for itself and she counted on her successes as a form of job security. She was dismayed to discover when the company was reorganized that her position was eliminated, and the new organization had no new role for her. Her solid performance had never worked against her, but apparently it hadn't worked for her, either. She walked away empty-handed after 10 loyal years.

The problem Renee encountered was that as much as she wanted her performance to count for everything, in her complex and changing organization, it didn't.

The problem company leaders faced was that even though they wanted to keep executive women in key roles, they couldn't.

Women like Renee felt suddenly at risk. They concluded that their organization didn't respect them and they, too, sought to leave. (This was no way to retain talented women.)

Does that mean all of Renee's hard work meant nothing? Hardly. Partly because of her excellence and reputation for results, she was well treated as she left and had amazing opportunities for what to do next. You can't always control what happens to you, but you *can* take steps to make sure good things do happen.

Working Twice as Hard for Half as Much

Performance becomes a dilemma for women when it doesn't seem to count the way it should. You do your best; you get great feedback; nothing happens.

It's a common experience, and research backs it up: both men and women report that whereas men only have to show *potential*, women are only promoted on their *performance*. In other words, the evidence shows that women, much more than men, must have proven accomplishments before their talent is recognized.[1]

The perfect performance environment would be a true meritocracy—a system in which people chosen to advance were selected on the basis of their ability. Performance isn't the only metric on which leaders are judged. But it is the most important.

The Performance Advantage

Unlike some of the other dilemmas we've discussed, performance is a clear indicator of success. The performance advantage is the understanding that when you deliver peak performance and showcase it appropriately, you have put the cornerstone into place for a successful career.

One executive whose career illustrates this is Marissa Mayer, the CEO of Yahoo. Mayer has a reputation for being laser focused on performance. When she described her perspective to us, Mayer was not focused on her own advancement, others' perceptions of her, or the challenges of corporate culture. She was predominantly focused on one thing: *results*. Her feeling was that when you have high goals and execute them well, you have choice as to what you want. It worked. In 2012, she was promoted to CEO of Yahoo and became a national presence.

You may have been focused on your performance all along, which is excellent. But leaders lose sight of this critical element of their success. There are several reasons.

1. **It may seem strange, but it's possible to miss the importance of performance.**
   Performance measures may not be clear in your organization, or maybe you're the one who's not entirely clear on those measures.
2. **You can become focused on the wrong thing—the next job, office politics, or the fire drill of the moment, instead of your results.**
   If you're not tracking your progress, it could be that no one else is, either.
3. **You can neglect to track changes in your performance measures over time.**
   Your performance measures change as your jobs change throughout your career. Be sure you're staying current.
4. **One final and potentially disastrous mistake is forgetting to identify, communicate, and improve your results.**
   You don't have to overdo it, but you *do* have to own your performance. No one else will do it for you.

For any of these reasons, you can neglect to prioritize performance. Maggie Wilderotter, CEO of Frontier Communications, says, "Performance is the ticket to the dance. Unless you're delivering results, there is no right to move forward."[2]

When it comes to your own performance, you are your own best advocate. You secure your performance by getting clear on the metrics that matter in your role—tracking the changes in those measures as your career progresses—and continuing to track your results.

The Benefits of Performance

The typical benefits of performance are pretty straightforward. This is, after all, what you're paid to do. Salary, benefits, and bonuses—these are all meant to compensate you for doing your job.

Beyond that, consider the additional rewards of doing your job *well*:

- Confidence.
- Marketability.
- Promotability.
- Career choice.
- Fulfillment.

Together, those rewards complete the picture of a fulfilling career.

If you show yourself to be a talented leader—and future leader—of your company, you can start gathering the experiences *now* that you'll need to succeed in the future. Then you won't just be promotable. You'll be prepared.

Our Perspectives

Howard

In my view, performance is the single biggest driver for advancement— or at least the one over which you have the most control.

There are so many other elements of your career you can't control. You can't control politics. You can't control timing. You can't control opportunity. You can't control the quality of your leader. (There are good ones and bad ones.) We know sometimes our success comes from being in the right place at the right time, and sometimes that's where we get our breakthrough, but you can't control how or when that will occur. The same is true of performance and promotion. You can't even control whether high performance will help you get ahead. In some cases, your manager may actually be afraid to put you in a new role because of how well you're performing in your current role!

You're smart to track your own performance, because it's one area you can control. As long as you're keeping track of your results, you have the information you need to go after better opportunities and upward mobility.

Measures (and Poor Measures) of Performance

As with all of our dilemmas, the performance dilemma is not exclusive to women. Men have to worry about it, too. But perhaps there is one area in which women tend to fare less well than men and that's when performance is mismeasured and misjudged.

Imagine you have two people, a woman and a man. Both are high performers. The man comes in at 7:00 a.m., wanders down to the café, hangs out talking for awhile, and eventually gets to his office and gets down to work around 9:00 a.m. He stops around noon, goes out to lunch, returns for meetings that start at 1:30 p.m., and works until 5:00 p.m. It's the end of the workday, and to take a break he wanders into the hall to see who's around as they wrap up their day, takes a break himself, and decides to get take-out and stay a little late. By 6:30 p.m. he's at his computer again and heads home around 8:00 p.m.

The woman comes in after dropping her kids off at 9:30 a.m., works through lunch and leaves at 5:00 p.m.

Who's put in a longer day?

I don't want to reinforce stereotypes here. In today's world, the man's and woman's roles could be reversed. The problem is many managers use face time as a measure of performance. The man in this example appears more present, because he *is* present—physically. He's in his office. He works long hours. The woman seems less committed. She's in late, she's never around because she's hunkered down in her office, and she leaves early. But if you count the hours, she's put in more work than the man.

The point is that "hours worked" is not a measure of performance nor are any number of poor measures such as personality, likeability, and assertiveness that serve as stand-ins when people don't take full responsibility for aligning performance to results. Performance should be judged on contributions made. Performance should always be linked to results.

Perceptions on Performance

How do you ensure you are being judged on your performance? You lead the conversation.

Let's say the issue is exactly as we've described it earlier, and you're afraid you're being misperceived by other people in your department. A meeting with your manager might sound like this.

"One of the concerns I have is that I get the feeling maybe some people, and maybe not even you, take a look at the fact that I come in at 9:30 and leave at 5:00 and judge it to be a lack of commitment to the organization. Do you feel that way?"

Regardless of their answer, you might continue.

"I want to be sure. Is everything you expect from the job getting done? Is there anything I'm not getting done?" You might even let your manager know you are getting things done when they're completely out of sight, like when you're working at night after taking care of your family, or early in the morning from home before you leave for work. Then ask your boss for support. "How can you help me make sure people don't end up with wrong idea?"

Engaging your manager is a big part of having your performance recognized. In this case, you want to create an advocate in your boss. When someone else puts forth a false assumption ("She does a phenomenal job, but she's divided in her loyalties."), you have an advocate who can correct the perception in your favor ("Actually, she's our highest performer.").

If you can confront the perceptions you don't want people to get about your performance, replace them with the perceptions you want them to have. Once again, this is an area in which you can take some initiative and control.

Proactive Performance Conversations

Once again, performance is about aligning behavior to results. It's not about checklists, boxes on forms, or annual reviews. It's an ongoing process of feedback and dialogue.

Unfortunately, even though organizations try to put structures into place to support this process, they don't always work. The performance review process is a good example. It's supposed to involve thoughtful goal setting. It's supposed to involve ongoing conversation. It's supposed to provide clarity and agreement. Too often all of that gets shelved. Instead you get a piece of paper called your "performance review" tossed at you near the water cooler with an off-hand remark: "Let me know if you have any questions."

Whether your company has a strong performance review process or not, you can be proactive about your performance. You *should* be proactive about your performance. You are the one accountable to your future and future development; you need to be the one who owns it.

It should be a substantive conversation with your boss, and it goes like this.

"I want to be sure I'm clear on the things you think are the best measures of my performance. How would you gauge my performance in my role?"

Be sure and ask for examples. Clarify. Check your understanding. Talk about where your strengths are and how to leverage those. Talk about what gets in your way and how you can work on that. Don't grill your boss; be a partner, so the two of you are completely in sync. You understand what your boss needs from you, and your boss knows you're clear on how to deliver.

Don't let this be a one-time conversation, now. Make a plan to benchmark your performance and return to your manager often. Share with him or her:

- Here's what we agreed I would do.
- Here's where I am now.
- What do you see as my next step?

Some organizations we work with are formalizing this process. Large, complex, global organizations are replacing old systems for performance review with ongoing, meaningful dialogue to support performance one-on-one and throughout the company—which is great news and signals a trend in which many more managers will be welcoming these conversations.

Conversations like these can take place no matter what your organization does in terms of performance reviews. One of my pet peeves is when companies want everyone to check off boxes on a form and consider that a decent review of performance. It's not. Performance is measured in the conversations that take place throughout the year. Central questions to gauge performance include "What are the contributions I'm making?" and "Where are my opportunities to do things differently or better?" Good performance results from honest feedback on the part of managers.

As a manager of yourself, you should also be modeling the conversations you wish your manager would have with you. By setting crisp, clear objectives, having the hard conversations, and focusing on your team development, you will start to create a culture of performance in which leaders like you can thrive.

Recognize that what it takes to succeed in this process draws on many of the other concepts in this book. Networking. Feedback. Advancement. That's why I believe that if you get really good at talking about, measuring, tracking, and communicating about your performance, many of the other dilemmas you face may fade away.

Joelle

There are three questions you can ask yourself to assess the impact of performance on your career:

1. Is performance emphasized where you work?
2. Which performance measures will you use?
3. How will you claim your results?

If you can get crystal clear in all three areas, you will be doing everything possible to make your good work count.

Let's take these one at a time.

Is Performance Emphasized Where You Work?

Pam Nicholson was the president and CEO of Enterprise. As she worked her way from management trainee up through the ranks—including positions as manager, regional vice president, and eventually president and CEO—she did it with her results.

> At Enterprise, we emphasize performance. We promote from within and only on performance. So even though the company was young and regional when I joined it, it looked like I would have opportunities in the future.

She confessed that she wasn't necessarily the type to brag about herself all the time, "so it was good to be in a place where performance would stand for itself." She said, "The beauty of my company is we measure everything. As long you can put your results on the table, the numbers will speak for themselves."

Your job is to know what those numbers are for you, and measure them.

Credibility Where It Counts

An old adage says that what gets measured, matters—and yet sometimes what's being measured isn't always clear. What are the measures of success for you?

- Sales results?
- The engagement of employees in your department?
- The satisfaction ratings of your clients or employees?
- The impact you make on market share?

- Your contribution to a high-profile, high-stakes project?
- Your ability to lead a strategic vision?
- The development of a high-performing team?
- Your ability to influence others without direct command and control?
- A variety of stakeholders' interests?

To this last point, different stakeholders to whom you're accountable may have different interests. That can indeed complicate your life.

You should be acutely attuned to how your performance is being measured and if you're not, ask your boss. If you're still not clear, do more digging. If you still can't get clarity, take a shot at it yourself—put together a list of the things you think you should be delivering and shop the list around to get a reaction. You have the right to expect to get an answer as to how you're being expected to perform.

But you're a high-achieving, high-performing leader. So let's think bigger. Beyond delivering on your current performance measures, are there goals you want to pursue?

- What's the next role you want, and what's required there?
- What have you already mastered, and how can you expand?
- Where are the gaps in your experience, and how can you fill them in?

A number of successful leaders have found that answering these questions can help them not just perform but also *out*perform their own expectations.

The shifts from one position to another, especially as you move up the ladder, require you to continuously revise what's expected of you. Your ability to do that, along with whatever other metrics you may be tracking, is an important measure of your performance.

Once you're clear on the measures of success, you can set out to claim your results.

Claiming Your Results

One comment I hear over and over from women is, "I don't like to toot my own horn." We want to know our results will matter. We want to have our good work recognized. There's only one thing wrong with assuming other people will celebrate your performance: if you don't tell them, how will they know?

This topic of getting your results recognized is so crucial that it qualifies as one of the dilemmas, and we'll look at it much more closely when we discuss the Recognition Advantage in the next chapter. For now, claiming your results is mostly about keeping your eye on those results and never losing sight of them.

Even if your company is exceptional at tracking and promoting on results, sometimes (for women, especially) those results aren't always prioritized. You may have to sing your own praises and point out how well you've been doing. You may have to advocate for yourself.

In short, the strategy is this: focus on performance, get the results, and make an effort to point out those results so you get the credit (and the opportunities) you have earned.

Q&A with Howard and Joelle

Is it really true that I might not get promoted because I'm "too good" at what I do?

Joelle: I have a feeling we struck fear into the hearts of some readers when they read their manager may actually be afraid to put them in a new role because of how well they're doing in their present role. I've heard that rumor in some of the organizations I've worked with, and is it ever de-motivating! What can a person do to avoid that?

Howard: In that case, the situation is entirely upside down. Your performance has actually become a disadvantage. If you suspect that to be true, I'd recommend a conversation. It might sound something like this:

"I'd like to follow up with you about the position in which I was interested. If you don't mind me asking, what is the reason I wasn't even considered for the job?"

If you have an inkling that your performance has backfired, you could say, "I want to understand. What you're saying is as long as I continue to do really well, I may not avail myself to opportunities. Is that right? It sounds as if I would do better to look for a position outside the organization. I want to work where I know I'll get credit for my performance. Do you see when I committed to this organization why that would be a problem?"

Joelle: There may actually be several reasons why it would be a problem, so keep an open mind. As much as I hate to say it, I've seen people who weren't as performing as well as they thought they were. They thought their department wouldn't let them move up because they were so good, but actually their department wouldn't let them up because they weren't as good as they thought they were. That's a painful discovery.

You can find out whether you're ready to move up simply by asking the question, but do so with a sense of humility and openness. What should be a creative and mutually beneficial ongoing conversation about performance can backfire when it's done poorly. You don't have to threaten. You don't have to whine. It won't go well if you try to force your way up. ("You said all I had to do to get promoted was to do these things!") You can't go into a "proactive performance conversation" with the intention to back your boss into a corner. Get the right perspective and plan your words.

There's at least one more reason a high-performing leader like you might not be promoted out of a department where you're needed, and that is there isn't a plan for your succession. You can get ahead of this. Anticipate that you'll want move up and need to be replaced, as early as two to three years in advance. Who will take over so you can move on? How can you groom that person to be ready? If your team is in great shape and can run the department without you, and if you have a good replacement, you will be in a better position to move on.

Just check it out with an open mind, and explore whether there is a possibility your career is being held captive by a department that needs your talents and doesn't want to lose you.

When I want my performance recognized and feel like it's not . . . what do I do?

Joelle: I heard a distinction once that people shouldn't think about being promoted but elected. Promotion means being given a new job by your company or manager. Election means being so strong and supported by everyone on a team that you're the natural and logical choice. Do you think that makes sense, and if so, does it point to a different measurement of success? In other words, if I want to be promoted I have to think about my performance . . . but if I want to be elected, am I still thinking about my performance or am I suddenly now focused on something else, like others' perception of me and my likeability factor?

Howard: I once worked with an executive who had always gotten results. Always. But the way he got results was he didn't suffer fools lightly. He got impatient with them. For years there were people who got promoted above him, because he didn't exhibit the whole package of what good leadership and good performance should mean.

In a way, it might sound like I'm arguing against myself! On one hand I say performance is all that matters, and then here's a story in which performance isn't enough! It's not the paradox it may seem. Again, of all the things that contribute to your advancement, performance is still only one. It's the only one that should matter. And it's the one you can control. You own your performance, and no one can take that away.

Joelle: No one can take that away . . . and perhaps you can even expand your influence. Let's say you have phenomenal results and feel like your performance isn't recognized, as you said in your question. You believe you're ready for a promotion, but have you thought about the notion of election? Beyond your results, do others see you as a leader? Would they put you forth as someone they wanted to lead them?

Election is not a popularity contest—it's a more expansive way of thinking about who gets the opportunity to lead. A peek behind the curtain about how people get promoted may be helpful. One of the senior executives who participated in our research described the process.

> Today I don't know anyone who's an executive vice president who doesn't consult with other EVPs in the organization about people on their team that they're thinking of promoting. Before someone goes from being a director to executive to an officer of the company, they are going to ask, how does your organization relate? Who is the one they put on complicated project, who is the one they want from their team to work on a particular initiative, who is the person they turn to when they're thinking about strategy?

The executives involved in that conversation are nominating names for the promotion. More than that—they're virtually electing them.

One more comment. To Howard's point, performance may be the most important factor for you emphasize. But in the words of one executive who learned this the hard way, performance can only get you so far. The rest of the matters in this book—strong executive presence, a powerful network, recognition for your results—these are also essential elements of your success.

How do I know I'm getting really good feedback on my performance—feedback I can trust?

Joelle: One of the things we've learned in our research at the Leadership Research Institute is that bad bosses can actually get in the way of good performance.

Howard: We have over 15 years of research at the Leadership Research Institute that backs that up. The data is all from interviews or surveys giving feedback to organizations, from a variety of industries, in variety of sizes, from around the world. The data shows that the four greatest areas of opportunities for managers all relate to talent:

1. Providing effective orientation on new tasks.
2. Providing effective coaching and feedback.

3. Leveling with employees about what's not negotiable.
4. Accepting constructive criticism.

In other words, managers largely fail on holding strong performance-related conversations, even though we know those conversations are a critical factor in employees' success!

Joelle: Our advice is for each individual leader to take ownership for his or her performance, partly because companies and managers generally don't do this well. We can help them. We can communicate what we need; we can ask for it; we can take ownership for scheduling the meetings and facilitating the conversation.

Howard: Right. If you need to be oriented to your job, you need clarity. If you need dialogue about your performance, ask for feedback. On those sometimes undiscussable issues (like executive presence and demeanor), open the discussion and make it safe.

Do I think managers should have to do a better job here? Yes, I do. Organizations could do a better job of expecting managers to develop their people well through high-quality performance reviews and ongoing feedback.

In the meantime, sometimes managers don't do this because they don't know how. They need the framework and the guidance that you can easily provide, to help them do this well—if not for all of their direct reports, at least for you. Sometimes the reasons managers don't have good conversations about performance is because they want to be nice—they don't want to offend. Or, maybe they're scared—they don't want to be sued. Your job is to make it as positive a conversation as possible by asking open questions and being ready to hear the answers.

Joelle: And deliver.

Cynthia: The End of the Story

Finally—*finally!*—the news came. Cynthia beamed as she announced her new position as corporate executive to the members of her mastermind:

"I wanted you to be the first to hear the news! I finally got the role I've been wanting!"

They cheered, then asked her, "What was it that finally made the difference?"

"This might not surprise you," she reported, "but we had a change in leadership. My old CEO finally moved on, and the new CEO came in with a fresh new perspective. We met several times. Finally—and I am

not making this up—he let loose on the board. 'What does it take for a woman to be promoted in this company?' were his exact words. I was promoted shortly after that."

"You know the lesson I learned? Never take your foot off the pedal. In my case, my hunch turned out to be right, at least according to the new CEO. It wasn't my imagination that the board wasn't promoting any women. They really weren't. It was only when the company changed and started attending to diversity and promoting based on performance that my results got the attention they deserved, but when things did change I was ready. My results had never changed; they were still the highest in the company. Now finally that performance has paid off."

As a result of her experience, Cynthia gained a nuanced understanding of the role of performance in her career.

She realized her performance didn't guarantee career advancement, but a lack of performance would have prevented it when the opportunity arose. In her case, the availability of those opportunities depended on a change in leadership. For other leaders, the availability of those opportunities might depend on timing, the other competitors for a position, and the needs of the organization. It was a lesson that helped her put performance in perspective.

"Perhaps more important than that, I didn't give up on myself. It would have been so easy to be bitter and resigned, and to slack off on my performance when it didn't seem to be paying off. But as I've always said, I love my work and I love this company. I didn't keep my performance up because I wanted the promotion. I kept it up because doing my best brings me joy."

Key Points

1. Using whatever outcomes matter most in your organization and your role, your performance is measured by your results.
2. Whereas women are promoted on their *performance*, men only have to show *potential*. In other words, the evidence shows that women, much more than men, must have proven accomplishments before their talent is recognized.
3. When you deliver peak performance and showcase it appropriately, you have put the cornerstone into place for a successful career.
4. Leaders lose sight of this critical element of their success.
5. When it comes to your own performance, you are your own best advocate.

Questions for Reflection

1. What are the performance measures on which you're judged?
2. Does your manager agree? How do you know?
3. Do you have concrete examples of results you've delivered and their importance to the organization?
4. How will you measure your own results and how will you communicate those results?

CHAPTER 6

The Recognition Advantage (How do you get your achievements noticed?)

"You need to own your career. Be very deliberate. You have to have the results and the credibility . . . It's always about delivering . . . But you need to raise your hand and ask. Because if you don't, someone else will."
— Mary Falvey, Executive Vice President and Chief Human Resources Officer, Wyndham Worldwide

Christine

Christine felt discouraged. She was a top producing realtor in a large commercial real estate company. She had multiple certifications in her industry and great relationships with both clients and senior management. She was anxious to be noticed for her successes, perhaps with a new title, an award, maybe a bonus, or a new opportunity. Instead, people got promoted all around her. Her turn never seemed to come. She started muttering to her friends that maybe it was time to change companies. Finally, desperate, she burst out in the middle of a sales meeting, "You work and work and work in this company, and no matter how well you do, no one seems to notice!"

From the back of the room, a senior executive stood up and offered to sponsor her to explore how she could expand her career.

Later in the hall, Christine thanked him. "I had no idea you'd want to sponsor me!" she exclaimed.

"I had no idea you were interested," he said. *"You never asked."*

Christine's story turned out well. With guidance from her new sponsor, within a few months she found herself spearheading a new initiative with visibility to the CEO. But what would have happened if she'd never spoken up? How many women walk away from their jobs in frustration and how many more give up trying and simply settle for staying where they are?

If you, like Christine, have ever felt that you are underappreciated, undervalued, or under leveraged; if you feel that your talents aren't being acknowledged to their fullest extent; if there are rewards, recognition, or positions that you want but never seem to get; then you know how she felt. You're doing everything you think you should be doing to excel, but no one seems to notice.

You can get yourself noticed at work. When you do, you'll gain the benefits and opportunities that come with knowing your value. We use this chapter to understand what it takes to get the attention you deserve.

The Recognition Dilemma

Recognition is about raising your hand, claiming credit for your work, volunteering yourself, and speaking up, so others notice your contributions and you create opportunities for yourself.

Even the most promising leaders may not get the recognition they're hoping for. One study shows that 61 percent of employees feel unappreciated at work.[1] Beyond the deflating effect this has on personal motivation, a lack of recognition also makes it difficult for organizations to identify who their top performers are, and rewards can seem random or unfair. Not good for company culture and not good for people, who after all want to know they're important and make a difference.

Beyond all of that, though, one of the reasons women, in particular, don't *get* recognition is that they don't *seek* recognition. They've learned not to.

- Women are often taught to (or tend to) deflect attention.
- Women are often taught to (or tend to) share the credit.
- Women are often discouraged from (or neglect to) claim their accomplishments.

These are patterns observed in women that have been reinforced throughout their lives.

- One study showed that women apply for open jobs only if they think they meet 100 percent of the criteria listed, whereas men respond to the posting if they feel they meet 60 percent of the requirements.[2]
- Another study found that although female employees are 8 percent more likely than men to meet or exceed performance expectations, they tend not to apply for promotion.[3]

Even when women are tapped by someone else for recognition, they don't always accept it.

To give an example, one of our client organizations started an initiative to expose top talent to senior leadership in which high-performing leaders throughout the company were pulled together and given a challenge to solve a business problem.

Even though the women selected for this program were handpicked for their potential, and even though this was a high-profile opportunity, and even though the women were heavily involved and worked quite hard on the project, when it came to the presentation to the CEO, the women sat down and let the men on their teams present. It happened over and over again.

There's no getting around it. If you want to be recognized, you need to go after it when the opportunity to be recognized presents itself.

Results don't always speak for themselves. Sometimes we have to speak for them.

Resolving this dilemma requires you to change your thinking. You'll need one part courage, one part initiative, and one part perspective. With an open mind and positive expectation, you can open new doors for yourself.

The Recognition Advantage

Women have a reputation for giving others credit—appreciating them and acknowledging them outwardly—sometimes even at the expense of themselves. In order for others to value you, you have to first value yourself. When you do, you'll gain the recognition advantage—the rewards and opportunities you've earned.

You may feel self-conscious shining a light on your accomplishments, but you don't have to be a braggart to be appropriately self-advocating. You can *be* yourself and still *get* yourself noticed.

There are a number of reasons besides your own credibility that you need your efforts to be noticed. You can lobby more effectively for your teams when you speak up. Your projects will get more support and your opinions will be heard. Your ability to shine a spotlight on your good work serves your own career, of course, but it also serves your company, your clients, and your team.

So yes, you'll have to be the one responsible for sharing your results, and that's not necessarily instinctual. Even in early childhood, little boys in a classroom have been shown to throw their hands in the air whether or not they know the answer ("Me! Me! Pick me!"), whereas little girls will sit quietly with their hands in their lap even if they have the right answer. Women need to undo that conditioning and learn to raise their hands—not just to ask but also to participate, to contribute, and to share successes.

Recognition is not about power grabbing and hogging air time. It's about challenging yourself to be more visible. You may have to practice—surprisingly, few leaders ever learn to accurately identify the right results, clearly articulate them, and communicate them to get a favorable reaction. But it's a learned skill, and you can master it.

In the words of Gail Kelman, director of leadership development at Guardian Life Insurance, "You can't consider speaking up as inauthentic or attention grabbing. You have own the fact that you have a unique set of skills and abilities that will drive the business results of the organization. It's your obligation as an associate to be sharing those observations, in a well thought-out way, with the people who are in a position to notice."

Raising your hand means taking a risk. You may be wrong. You might be labeled as overaggressive or overly ambitious. Yet, many women have learned that sitting with your hands quietly folded in your lap is the best way to go unnoticed.

Recognition comes when you achieve what's important to the people around you and highlight the wins. Your ability to call attention to your achievements and ask for what you need will serve your career. You don't have to overdo it. Just make sure you don't avoid doing it at all.

HOW TO TAKE CREDIT

Getting credit is often about *taking* credit. Others won't necessarily recognize what you've done without you telling them. You have to show them what you're doing that's worth noticing. Consider what other leaders have learned about what works in taking credit.

1. **Share your activity.**
   "This week I'm working hard on a number of priorities. To give you a sense of where I'm putting my attention, these are some of the things I'm doing . . ."
2. **Share your accomplishments.**
   "I'm pleased to report the accomplishments I've made in this area . . ."
3. **Create a synopsis or report.**
   "I knew you'd want to know how things turned out, so I've summarized some thoughts and data we can go through together."
4. **Ask for positive feedback.**
   "Feedback is important to me. I want to be sure I'm on track. Tell me, where do you think I'm doing a good job, and where do you think I've been most effective?"
5. **When others take credit for your work or ideas, correct the record.**
   "Let's revisit history. I'm so glad this new initiative has worked out, and a lot of people deserve the credit for its success! Do you remember that was originally my idea?"
6. **Think your ideas through.**
   A half-baked idea can be finished and carried forward by someone else. A fully baked idea is complete and deserves the credit. Do some planning about how to carry your idea forward, and bring additional details, data, and anecdotes to show how your plan can be fully implemented.
7. **Announce your ideas in public.**
   Share your thinking and ideas out loud, not just quietly to a colleague (or not at all). In the words of Huffington Post columnist Jennifer Winter, "Though it might be intimidating, announcing your plans to a wider audience naturally helps prevent others from being tempted to 'borrow' or 'be inspired by' your ideas."[4]

The Benefits of Recognition

For many women, recognition is a reward in itself. Women want their good performance celebrated, and recognition by management and peers of their contribution to the organization is a source of validation and fulfillment.[5]

Being recognized as leader can lead to other rewards, as well. By high-lighting your accomplishments, you can gain:

- Stretch assignments.
- Recognition for your capabilities and successes.
- The opportunity to join high-visibility or high-interest projects.
- Rewards for your results.
- Promotions.

In addition to you benefitting from getting yourself recognized, your company receives the benefit through increased engagement. Companies with a "recognition-rich culture" have a 31 percent lower turnover rate—which is important for women, who reportedly value "appreciation by their manager" 15 percent over men as an important reward for their work.[6]

Our Perspectives

Howard

I have a few strategies to share that can aid your efforts to gain recognition. The first one I call signposting. The second is how you present your-self. The third is knowing what others value.

Signposting

To reiterate the importance of performance, the quickest way to get noticed is to get something accomplished that no one else has been able to do. But there's an additional piece to performance that ensures you actually get your good work recognized. You have to point it out.

One strategy you can use to do this is what I call signposting. You tell people exactly what you did so they can recognize it. It sounds like this:

> "As you know, I've been working on increasing our revenue. I'm pleased to announce in the last quarter I raised our revenue 8 percent."
>
> "It's important to me to have a high-performing team. I've noticed as a result of the performance initiatives I've implemented this year, my team's productivity improved significantly."
>
> "You'll see our team has succeeded in bringing in several new clients. I'm proud of their efforts. I've made it a priority to focus their attention and make sure they had the resources to get there, and they did."

Signposting doesn't mean you brag about yourself and take all the credit. In a team effort, you may very well acknowledge that the team gets the credit and that they made the difference. But you can also make it clear as to who enabled that to happen.

Substance vs. Bluster

It's important when we talk about taking credit or getting noticed that we get the message right.

One of the executives we've worked with who has observed differences in the way men and women do this is Tony Nugent. Nugent is an executive vice president from MetLife who has arranged a biannual gathering of top saleswomen, the Women's Sales Summit, to develop them and help them advance. Standing in the room—the only man among 100 women—he noticed the women were sometimes waiting to be selected for promotions as opposed to going out and claiming them for themselves.

> I learned that they are expecting us to tap them on the shoulder. I was surprised. There are a couple of jobs open this week, and the guys call and say, "I want that job!" And they're not even great candidates! We were able to accomplish helping the women at the Women's Sales Summit think about their career a different way—to realize it's their responsibility to step up. One woman came up to me afterward and did that. She said, "I'm ready now to move up in my career. I want to do more."

Nugent makes a couple of good points. One, you have to take responsibility for getting noticed and expressing what you want, and two, you need to be qualified when you do so.

Some people do this badly. They may take credit they don't deserve or make their results seem better than they are. You have to have the substance to back up your claims.

Does that mean a little bit of buzz doesn't matter? Not necessarily. If people don't know you very well, they may respond to your enthusiasm and the impression you make. The excitement you create around your ideas can draw attention to your ideas. On the other hand, if you have a brilliant mind and game-changing ideas but you are awkward in conveying the message, people may get distracted and overlook the substance. It's another reason why executive presence isn't something to be ignored.

But neither is it enough. The goal is to have substance, presented well—the brilliance and the buzz. Some people have exceptional performance that goes unnoticed. Some people get all the attention but don't deliver. You need to do both.

Knowing What Others Value

In order to get recognition from others, you need to know what they're looking for and what they will count as success.

For example, I know myself to be someone who looks for substance. It doesn't matter how slick the presentation is or how polished the presenter. If I see someone speaking at a meeting who doesn't know what they're talking about, nothing else will matter in my mind. But the presentation style might matter to others. It's not just what matters *to you* that gets you noticed. It's what matters to the person you want to do the noticing.

Let's say you want to impress a group of leaders in a meeting. Some of those leaders may be thoroughly wowed by fancy materials, catchy slogans, and big words. Some of those leaders might be drawn to your charisma. Perhaps there are leaders in the group who place the most value on your ability to take the ball and run with it on your own. Or maybe there are leaders who are looking for you to involve the group and facilitate a discussion. There might be a leader who would be most impressed if you stopped by after the meeting to follow through on a question.

If you don't know what matters to a person, how can you find out?

1. **Be receptive.** Notice what people respond to and what they seem to value.
2. **Put yourself in their shoes.** If you want to know something about a customer, you don't read up on their company. You read up on the industry. Understand what their concerns and goals are. Understand what drives them. The same is true in the settings in which you want to get noticed. What's valued there? What do people seem to care about?
3. **Ask the person directly what's most important to them.** You can view this as a sign of respect. Your goal is to calibrate your efforts to the people who matter most to you. In order to do that you can ask them for direction. Ask them what's important to them and pose a few follow-up questions.

By taking these steps, you'll make an impression on the people you want to notice you. You will develop your relationship with them while understanding more about how you can stand out in their minds.

When you consciously show people why you deserve attention and what you want them to see, present it in a way that is both appealing and meaningful, and direct your message to what others care about most, you put yourself in the best position to be recognized.

Joelle

To get noticed, you need to *know* and *show* your value.

Knowing Your Value

Raising your hand hinges on an important foundation: knowing your value.

Mika Brzezinski, coanchor of MSNBC's *Morning Joe* and author of *Knowing Your Value* has some fascinating (and scary) stories about the money, opportunities, and rewards women have left on the table by not knowing their value. For a while, she was one of them. When she found out exactly what she was being paid relative to her male counterpart, Joe Scarborough—*fourteen times* less—she put her foot down and made a different choice.

She quit. Only then did MSNBC, at the vehement prodding of Scarborough himself, acknowledge Brzezinski's value to the program and offer her a better deal.[7]

There are details of Brzezinski's experience that may be unsettling. (Do you actually have to quit your job before someone will finally notice your value? Does it really still take a man lobbying for you to be paid what you're worth?) The fact remains that the impetus for Brzezinski's raise and promotion started with *her* efforts to be recognized.

Do you know your value? How would you measure it? If you're someone who sometimes feels like you're not being recognized and you're ready to take the initiative to make some things happen, take stock of your accomplishments. What skills have you mastered? What talents do you bring? Where have you made progress? What achievements have you made? What results have you achieved? What's your market value? Knowing these things, you prove your value to yourself, so you can take a stand for what you have earned.

On the other hand, we might want to recognize that women sometimes spend more on this self-assurance than is necessary. The advice I like best comes from a CEO in her late 50s. "In the end, we don't have a lot of time to waste. Waiting around for someone to validate whether you should be in a role . . . forget it. Just go out and get it."

Raising Your Hand

If you want to be promoted, recognized, or supported in any way as a leader, you're going to have to raise your hand. Business environments are often skewed toward an extroverted, typically male, put-yourself-out-there ("Coach, Coach, put me in!") kind of culture, and if you want to be a part of it, you'll have to speak up.

You may hesitate to do this, especially if you have a quieter leadership style. Take heart—you're not alone. Many leaders would naturally prefer to sit back and listen, or speak only when they have something worthwhile to say, or would rather communicate behind the scenes where the pace is slower and more thoughtful.[8] Those are all options, and you may choose to engage in a quieter way, but you do have to participate. You can't stay in the background if you want to be noticed.

What could raising your hand look like?

- Asking for stretch assignments.
- Promoting your big wins.
- Connecting your efforts to good results.
- Volunteering for opportunities.
- Nominating yourself for advancement.
- Demonstrating your capabilities.
- Sharing your point of view.
- Having an opinion.
- Putting forth a perspective.
- Asking a question.
- Moving a discussion forward.
- Raising an important point.
- Challenging an assumption.
- Proposing an idea.
- Providing some data.
- Clarifying expectations.
- Taking the lead on a project.

The list goes on. Getting recognized is stepping up, getting involved, and being visible. What could you be sacrificing by not speaking up?

In those situations when you have the opportunity to raise your hand, whether it's a committee meeting or a board meeting or an opportune moment in time, remember that little girl sitting quietly with her hands in her lap and have the courage to put your hand up, even if you don't feel ready. The funny thing about the research on little boys is that after all their "Ooh! Oohing" and stretching themselves out of their seats, when their teachers finally call on them they often don't even know the answer. You do. Raise your hand.

Don't Let Yourself Be Marginalized

We've talked about what you can do to get yourself noticed, as well as how you present your good work so that others notice you. There will still be situations in which you not only feel *not recognized* but you also actually feel *marginalized.*

Several executives in our research had advice on how to respond.

- One noticed a pattern in her company in which men made lateral moves into existing positions, but when women made lateral moves, the title and compensation of the existing job were lowered before they took it. She made a decision never to take a job she didn't consider on par with her male counterparts in terms of salary, title, and reporting structure.
- Another commented that she'd seen too many women get coerced into accepting unfavorable roles. "You want to be asked to join the team, but you don't want to be the water boy. You want to be the quarterback." She made a commitment to herself to take assignments where she could add real value—not just do the work.
- A third said, "When you feel you're being pushed into the background, you need to take action to put yourself in the forefront. You have to claim back your position." She became more mindful about when she felt excluded and used those moments to take a stronger stance as a leader.

As a reminder, we don't want to blame anyone for the way these events play out, especially because so many companies are working hard to instill an ethic of equality. In addition to not letting yourself be marginalized, be sure you don't marginalize *yourself.*

When someone recognizes a contribution you've made, stop and thank them. Acknowledge what you've done. Many women rush so fast into acknowledging others ("No, really, it was the team that did it!") that they take themselves completely out of the picture—as if they had no hand in the success. You can take the credit you deserve while at the same time acknowledging your role in getting the results ("Thank you! I appreciate you acknowledging that. Yes, I'm pleased with the results. The entire team was also instrumental in making that happen.")

Q&A with Howard and Joelle

You say the research shows boys "raise their hands" more than women, but it seems to me women are very participatory. Is that a contradiction?

Howard: What's interesting to me is that my experience doesn't always match up with the research. When I think back to my school days, I recall the girls being the ones who always had the answers, and the teachers had to say, "Let's give everybody a chance!" Is that the difference between a work setting and an academic setting? Is it the difference between a group setting and an individual setting? Or could it be that this tendency for women to sit on their hands is really just a result of being in the minority—the only woman at the table?

I think about groups of leaders I've worked with in organizations that were made up only of women. They had plenty to say!

Joelle: If we take for a moment the premise that perhaps what's intimidating is being the only woman in a strongly male setting, with male norms and a male culture, then the issue becomes one of confidence and learning (or challenging!) the rules. You can take part in the culture by engaging in a different way than you normally do—say, by taking part in a debate over an important issue or contributing new ideas to a discussion. Or you influence the culture by doing things your way, even if they represent a departure from the way a group normally operates. I've seen both men and women who sit back and listen more than they talk. When they finally speak up, you can hear a pin drop, because when they talk they have something meaningful to say. Often in a group like that the other people will learn to value all the voices.

What doesn't make sense is to sit quietly in the back of the room while everyone else jockeys loudly for position. There's nothing powerful about sitting in the back and hoping to be recognized. You may choose that if it's your style, but you won't get the results you want.

Howard: Neither will you get the results you want if you only interact in situations that don't stretch you. Sometimes women only interact with other women.

Joelle: In a group of women, where the norms and culture derive from a feminine approach, getting noticed may not even be an issue. Women love to work together, collaborate, acknowledge each other, and yes, give each other credit. We tend to share the wealth. It's not always our nature to point out what we've done best. We'd rather celebrate what we've done together, as a group. It's one reason I'm an advocate for women's groups.

Howard: And it's one reason I'm not. You can get too comfortable, and how does that help? Put it this way. If an executive woman gets all the accolades from the women around her and then exits the room into a male-dominated culture, what has she done to get noticed in the settings managed by men? I'm actually surprised so many women's groups only look to women for their speakers and sponsors. They would learn a lot by getting the different perspective a man might bring.

Joelle: And so would he. So often the leadership development programs I lead are sponsored by men, but facilitated by women. I always want to make sure men have a presence in the room, if only at the beginning of the program, so he can experience what it's like to be a woman in the company, and so they can learn from a man's point of view. Women can learn from women, women can learn from men, and vice versa.

When it comes to getting recognized, the norms and values of the culture are critical to understand so you know your message will be heard.

I've been told by my executive coach and my sponsor that I need to take credit for my successes . . . but my boss tells me not to worry so much about taking credit and to let others shine. It's another dilemma!

Joelle: One of the reasons this topic ended up in this chapter is because so many women are stuck in this predicament. They've heard they need to step up, get noticed, get out there, and get in there. But that's not really their style. That's dilemma number one: either be bold and blustery or be ignored.

They've also discovered that when they do try to take credit, it backfires. They're accused of grabbing all the glory and not being a team player. That's dilemma number two: either say something and be blamed, or say nothing and let others take the credit.

Howard: We talked about several things you can do to get noticed. You have the results. You have the relationship with the person you want to notice you. All of those things you can control. What you can't control is the willingness of the other person to accept and see what you're doing.

Joelle: True. I suppose it only takes a little bit of negative feedback to understand if you're striking the wrong chord. If it's important for women not to blend into the background, they're going to have to take some risks, and taking risks means making mistakes. My counsel would be to be attuned to the way people respond to you, and ask for feedback. You can never underestimate the power of information and self-awareness.

Howard: Nor can you underestimate (once again) the power of performance. If you over-deliver in an area of impact, as long as you don't bury the results, you're well on your way to building a reputation you can be proud of.

Why should I have to get myself recognized? Why shouldn't my work speak for itself?

Joelle: Sometimes it strikes women as offensive that they may have to point something out to their manager that they've achieved ("I shouldn't have to point it out! He should just notice!")

Howard: Pointing out the obvious—or signposting, if we want to call it that—isn't cheating. Focus on the outcome. Is it more important to you that others notice you or that they notice you on their own? What really matters?

Joelle: In a busy work environment, things are not only complex but constantly moving and changing. Layer on top of that the fact that people are wrapped up in their own concerns and it's a wonder they *ever* notice the good that we do. Their heads are down, buried in their own work and lives.

We can lift their chins, look into their eyes and focus their attention on what we want them to see. If we don't take responsibility for doing that, we may be contributing to our tendency to be missed.

Christine: The End of the Story

Christine had gotten so frustrated about the lack of recognition coming her way that she snapped. Speaking out in an outburst during the sales meeting might not have been the most diplomatic move, but it resulted in her getting a sponsor and eventually a boost to her career. It also taught her a valuable lesson—one that was learned by all of the women in the room.

"I had worked myself into such a frenzy that I snapped," Christine admitted. "I was just so discouraged. When my sponsor told me the reason I hadn't been noticed was because I hadn't asked, I suddenly realized he was right. All that time I was waiting for someone to notice me, but I wasn't actually showing up in a way that would get me noticed."

"I noticed the same thing," said Christine's colleague. "When Christine's sponsor stood up and publicly offered his support, the world stood still. It was as if every woman in the room breathed a collective, 'Oh.' We suddenly got the message—it was only because Christine spoke up that she got noticed, and as soon as she did speak up, the doors opened for

her. The impact was immediate. I and two other women at my table went over and talked to our managers about what we needed that very same day!"

Also in the room that day was the head of learning and development for the company.

"It taught me a valuable lesson, too," he said. "We don't teach people that skill here. It was only from Christine that I discovered how many women are waiting patiently in silence, toiling away and getting amazing results but never getting ahead. We have some cultural changes to make in our company so that it doesn't have to get to the point where someone is about ready to snap, like Christine was, or where they feel hidden. Even though we want our talented women to stand up for themselves, they shouldn't feel they have to bang on the table to be heard, and we don't want them thinking if they don't bang on the table they'll have to leave the company to get a better opportunity. We need to open the lines of communication and promotion both ways so the right people get recognized."

Key Points

1. Recognition is about raising your hand, claiming credit for your work, volunteering yourself, and speaking up, so that others value your contributions and you create opportunities for yourself.
2. Results don't always speak for themselves. Sometimes we have to speak for them.
3. You can *be* yourself and still *get* yourself noticed.
4. In order for others to value you, you have to first value yourself.
5. Recognition comes when you achieve what's important to the people around you and highlight the wins.

Questions for Reflection

1. What do you want to be recognized *for*? Why?
2. Who do you want to recognize what you've done? What's important to that person to know, see, and hear?
3. How do you want to be recognized?
4. Have your results been noticed so far? What has been the result?
5. What can you do to help others recognize, appreciate, and reward your contribution?
6. What changes in your own behavior might you need to make to effectively get recognition?

CHAPTER 7

The Advancement Advantage (How do you turn your accomplishments into career advancement?)

"Am I ambitious enough to say I'm looking for more? Yes, as long as that allows me to have a rewarding personal life. I have peace, and it's an intrinsic value that's sometimes worth more than the money."

—Christa Carone, former Chief Marketing Officer, Xerox

Heidi and Jen

Heidi and Jen sat at a table at their company's Women's Leadership Forum—a national event hosted by their company specifically for the purpose of promoting the career growth of future leaders. They had just heard an inspiring message from the executive sponsor of the event, a president named Robert Montreaux. Robert had said he believed in them and wanted them to succeed and that he personally would do anything he could to help them grow their careers.

"I know Robert wants us to move up," said Heidi. "That would be great if Robert was my boss. If this company wants to support its women, my manager never got the memo. He barely even posts his positions. He just looks around and picks the guy for the next position—usually someone just like him."

"I have the opposite problem," said Jen. "Not only does my manager want me to move up, he basically isn't giving me a choice. He told me recently, 'You're at the top now in sales. Unless you want to retire in this role, you'll have to do something different.' I was shocked. I like sales.

I like the flexibility, the systems I've developed, and the income. The only way to advance from here would be to go into management, and management at that level means grueling travel and endless dinner meetings. I have a baby and a two-year old son! I don't want that! Here I thought I'd found the perfect job where I could have the flexibility and the income, but that's not how my boss sees things at all. He actually said to me, 'I've given you every advantage to get you ready for this. If I thought this was all you wanted to do, I wouldn't invest the time in you.'"

Do women want to move up, or don't they? If they do want to advance, how do they? If they don't want to advance, why don't they? The questions about advancement for women in leadership are multiple and complex.

- Some women want to move up but never do.
- Some women love the job they have but feel pressured to move up.
- Some women want to move up, but not right now.

They can't say yes, and they can't say no. The scenarios are particular to every woman and always shaped by the culture and structures of the companies for which they work.

The questions about why more women don't lead big corporations is a societal, even a global issue. We can explore some of the confusion you might encounter and attempt to provide some direction and clarity so you can make your own decisions about what's right for you. We can't promise you'll get every position you ever want the moment you want it, but we can offer some guidance as to how you can influence the outcome.

Ideally, you'll feel some reassurance that your best efforts will pay off. In this chapter, we look at options for how you can advance as high and as fast as you want into success as you define it.

The Advancement Dilemma

Advancement in this chapter primarily means being promoted, especially at the top of the organization and above the infamous line where women's careers tend to stop. It can also mean moving successfully into a new phase in your career, which may or may not include the traditional corporate image of promotion.

Even though all ambitious leaders have career advancement on their minds, for women it can be clouded with doubt. First, businesswomen are not advancing the way they want to—at the time and into the roles they believe they have earned and that suits their vision for their lives—

and that creates a level of worry and stress about whether it's even possible. Second, if it is possible, women don't always know *how* to break through to the next level—or even *if* they want to.

Resolving this dilemma means choosing your perspective on moving up—one that makes you to feel empowered and inspired. But first, let's look at a couple of perspectives that *don't* work.

The Tiara Syndrome

One of the paths to advancement that doesn't work is waiting for it to arrive on a silver platter. Author Rebecca Shambaugh calls it "the tiara syndrome"—waiting for someone to crown you and give you the promotion rather than telling someone else you want the next opportunity.

You can avoid the tiara syndrome by taking the lead in your own career and making things happen. Little girls learn early on that happy endings come when Prince Charming appears and sweeps the pretty girl off to the castle. High-achieving women come to understand they can write their own happy endings for themselves.

Ambivalence

The other path that doesn't work is playing a passive role as the events unfold in your life. Many women get stuck in ambivalence about whether and how they want to move up. Do I lean in or lean out? Scale up or scale back? Uncertainty can lead to a sense of powerlessness, which makes it less likely to happen, which only feeds further into doubt and fear. You have plenty of choice as to how you design your life and career. You can choose if and when you want that next big promotion. You get to define success for yourself.

While you're at it, consider that success may mean much more to you than the next promotion. Forbes blogger Peggy Drexler says women have a more well-rounded view of success.

> What do working women want? They want equal pay. Supportive mentors. More opportunity to hold positions of power. Flexibility. An end to the need for gender quotas. They want to be heard. Working women also want balance. They want to lean in, but they want to be able to tuck their kids in at night. They don't want to feel exhausted all the time. They want to get to the gym, or for a manicure, or for a spontaneous afternoon getaway with a friend or partner without making apologies or feeling guilty.[1]

Success means different things to different people. You will feel clearer about how to attain your aspirations when you can resolve any ambivalence you may have, define what "advancement" means for you, and go after it without feeling apologetic or pressured about what it is you "should" want.

Women want different things out of their lives and careers. That's your prerogative. In our executive coaching, we see the pressures and anxieties melt away—and the motivation return—when women discover their genuine hopes for their lives and set the intention to get it.

Elease Wright, the senior vice president of Human Resources for Aetna, suggests that to be successful in the ways that are important to you, you've got to get control over the events of your career.

> You can't wait for something to happen to you, just hoping that someone somewhere will say, "I see potential in this person—I'll go develop them." You have to figure out what you can take ownership of yourself.

As Shipman and Kay say in *Womenomics*, "The simple (but critical) knowledge that you can structure your career the way you want, that you do have real power, can literally change your life."[2]

The Advancement Advantage

The advancement advantage that can be a breakthrough for women is understanding the unlimited opportunities available to them when they expand their awareness of what "advancement" means. With an enlightened perspective about what success and achievement mean to you, you will finally understand what women mean when they say they have it all. You just may have it all, too.

But let's be clear about what we mean by "having it all." Shipman and Kay call it the "New All"—*enough* professional success, balanced by time and freedom.

> The overwhelming majority of women are longing to kick down that dreaded corporate ladder . . . but at the same time hold onto some real status . . . We want to use our brains and be productive professionally, but we don't want to keep tearing at the fabric of our families or our lives . . . We want to slow down . . . We'd like to spend our time at work engaged in meaningful and fulfilling pursuits . . . We will trade duties, a title—even salary increases—for more time, freedom, and harmony.[3]

As encouragement to hold out for the New All, they remind women how valuable they are:

> Women top every company's most wanted list. . . . Why? Because businesses with more women in senior positions make more money. It's as straightforward and stunning as that.[4]

The point is you have choice. You have latitude and leverage. What will you do with it? Will you create the life you want?

If the answer to that question is *yes,* you have two steps to take. One, you have to get clarity on what you want. Two, you have to *communicate.* Leaders and their managers often make assumptions about advancement, and that can lead to exasperation on both sides.

- Women assume their managers know they want to advance; know *how* they want to advance and how they don't; and know when they are ready for that next career move.
- Managers may assume women want the same things they do *or* they may make assumptions about what women want that aren't true for the women they lead.

With this in mind, think about your advancement strategically. Be clear about what you want, prepare for it, ask for it, expect a positive outcome, and persist. Stay positive and optimistic. From promotions to status to the next level title to the next big raise—or maybe a more creative option, like a shared leadership role, more freedom or flexibility—you can create the opportunities you have in mind for yourself and for your life.

WHAT WOMEN WANT

The traditional rewards for succeeding in business are well established.

- Career advancement.
- A high income.
- Power and status.
- Job security.

But are those the rewards that are right for *you?* As you consider your goals for yourself, we encourage you to think broadly about what you're trying to achieve—not just as a leader but also across your life.

In addition to the traditional rewards, women have an extra list of what they want from their work:

1. Strong, professional relationships with people they respect.
2. A more balanced lifestyle, including flexibility in work arrangements.
3. Genuine sponsorship and mentoring opportunities.
4. Authenticity ("the ability to be myself").
5. A merit-based culture.
6. Recognition and appreciation from their companies.
7. A sense of meaning and fulfillment in their work.
8. Developmental opportunities.
9. A fair and balanced workplace.

What do *you* really want?

The Benefits of Advancement (Traditional Definition)

If you're a talented, ambitious leader, the Big Promotion may be your endgame—the ultimate reward.

Traditionally, getting a promotion has been assumed to be the marker of success, bringing with it an uptick in:

Financial Rewards.
Status.
Power or Authority.

You'll also get to celebrate that incredible sense of recognition and accomplishment that comes from reaching a big goal and being recognized by others. All of that is great—when it happens, and if it happens, for the fewer and fewer positions in an organization found at the top.

The problems with the rewards of moving up as it is traditionally defined—as being promoted—are multiple:

• They are reserved for an increasingly small number of people, the higher one looks on the company org chart.

- They are contingent on the whims of organizational change and subject to many factors out of your control, including the hiring manager's preferences, the needs and specifics of the role, and politics.
- They fail to incorporate other benefits important to leaders, who in addition to money, status, and power may be looking for benefits related to their responsibilities, a sense of meaning and enthusiasm, and their autonomy.

In other words, before you hang your sense of success on the title on your door, it may be worthwhile to expand your definition of success.

The Benefits of Advancement (Expanded Definition)

For many leaders, getting a promotion doesn't end up bringing the career satisfaction or happiness they anticipate. Or, the experience of *not* getting a promotion brings down their confidence and can actually limit their ability to keep reaching for the next level of success.

You can redefine success so it captures all of the benefits that are important to you. For instance, it may be that "advancing" isn't so much about status for you as it is about gaining a greater sense of respect, exceeding your own expectations, feeling a sense of fulfillment, or raising the engagement scores of your team. "Advancing" may not have to do exclusively with a title and position, but with the opportunity to build a winning team, add responsibilities, have a positive impact on the organization, or work in a certain area of the business that's exciting to you. "Advancing" may not have to do with money for you, but rather the ability to assert some control over your schedule, location, and assignments, so you have a greater sense of balance and joy across your life.

What's the big win for you? What are all the many additional benefits that will bring?

Our Perspectives

Howard

I think both men and women sometimes go looking for a path for promotion when the answer is right before them. The only variable you can be confident in is the results you manage to produce. There are a lot of variables that may not be fair but as the old saying goes . . . life is not fair. Focus instead on the things you can control.

Setting a New Standard

I believe the best way to reach your potential is to set a standard that is just plain hard to ignore. This does not mean you will always get promoted. There are plenty of reasons you may not. It does mean you can be confident that you did the very best you could. Perhaps that's all any of us can really do.

All too often, I have seen people who are more focused on their next promotion rather than the job they have currently. If someone does not want to promote you, don't give them ammunition—give yourself ammunition in the form of great results. Even if it does not work where you are, look at what it will do for your job search.

You're much better off focusing on overachieving in your current position. Get results that are so stellar they simply can't be ignored. Make it difficult for people to overlook you. There is no better way to get job fulfillment than performing at a level that becomes the new standard for the position.

I have numerous times in my life promoted women who I believed had potential far beyond a natural progression. Each time, I came under extreme pressure for my judgment skills, including almost harassment when I recruited a woman who was five months pregnant. I was happy to take the risk, since I believed none of these women would have proved me wrong. They did not. It was amazing how everyone around me took credit when they demonstrated their value! Being the best you can be, even to the point of surprising others, is the way to be recognized and advance.

Staying the Course

The flip side to being your best is, unfortunately, realizing that your best may not be enough to move ahead. There are many reasons you may not be promoted despite your results.

Everyone has favorites. Sometimes they hide them, or sometimes they are in-your-face obvious. These favorites can be based on gender, race, personality type, similar hobbies, and any number of other factors completely out of your control.

Companies often have a succession plan that in the end they ignore. One of the things I learned after being responsible for succession planning in organizations is that the most well thought-out plans do not always come through. The organization would spend months reviewing the succession of a variety of roles and build great looking charts. Then, when a vacancy occurred, the hiring manager would look at the person he or she felt the best about and pick him or her, without a rational process and without consulting the succession plan.

So again, the decisions made around promotions are not always fair.

This is an area where men and women approach the problem differently. Men get ticked off, maybe they can see the leader picked their favorite candidate over them, they think the decision was wrong, and yet they still clearly believe the decision was not personal. My perception of women who do not get the job is they believe they should have done more, there is something the hiring manager questioned about their ability to succeed, and if they had been better connected, they would have gotten the role. Either may be right. Perhaps the most effective response is a bit of both—to reflect on the experience and see what there is to learn, then quickly move on and go back to focusing on your results.

There is no antidote for bad decisions. Sometimes the right person is picked for the wrong reasons; sometimes the wrong person is picked for the right reasons. Only sometimes is the right person picked for the right reasons. Remembering this can keep you from beating yourself up and allow you to keep moving forward.

Choosing Your Perspective

There's a middle ground between the right decisions ("You performed best! You got the job!") and the wrong decisions ("You performed best! But you didn't get the job"). We can call it simply "other decisions." They're not right or wrong, they just are the way they are. You have a lot of latitude as to how you handle them. You will come through these situations in the most productive way if you choose a healthy perspective on the decisions.

For instance, one time I was given an opportunity to take a job in London, Ontario. It would have been a promotion, but I didn't want to move to London, Ontario, so I didn't get the job. Was it fair or unfair? It doesn't matter; it just was the way it was. I was happy where I was, I was pleased to have been offered the promotion, but I realized that it was my choice to take a stand on the issue of moving location, and I accepted the consequences. Two years later I was offered a promotion again, this time in Toronto, and I was fine with that, so I took it. I realized I couldn't expect the organization to change the rules for me, so I just kept working hard and producing phenomenal results. Eventually, the organization bent to me.

There was another time I was by far the best candidate for a promotion. I didn't get it. I was told, "We're not ready for you yet." Was it fair or unfair? Again, it's not a question that really matters. Looking back,

I can see they were right. I would have been miserable in that role. I would have stirred up the organization and it wouldn't have been good.

In one more instance, I can think of a woman who was so focused on promotion that she got herself promoted too soon. She achieved phenomenal results—far better than any other man or woman. She was promoted solely on the basis of those results and no other measure of performance. She ended up being the worst person to promote, because she was so focused on herself and results, and she didn't have the breadth of leadership skills needed for the position.

In each of these instances, the question isn't just, "Have I performed the best?" Nor is it, "Is this situation fair or unfair?" The question is, "How I can look at this situation in a way that helps me stay motivated and committed to my goals?"

My strong bias, if you want to move up, is to set a new standard of excellence for the position you're in. Do your best in course of your career, while at the same time being aware that performance is not the only factor. You can avoid the frustration if you choose to let it go and get back to the business of developing yourself.

Joelle

Remember the definition we proposed at the beginning of this chapter for advancement, as moving up in your career—possibly with a promotion, but also in other ways that may be equally beneficial.

1. What does advancement mean to you?
2. What will determine the result?
3. What else matters to you?

Let's discuss each of these questions.

What Does Advancement Mean to You?

The notion that "advancement" may mean more than a promotion may be new to you, especially if you have your sights set on a seat one level up. But what else is there? Are there other ways of advancing that would excite you and advance your career? Let me give you some examples of what else advancement might mean.

Flexibility. Advancement might mean more flexibility: you've earned the respect and trust of your organization, and you are rewarded with the opportunity to work in the way that works best for you and the rest of your life.

Opportunity. Advancement might mean opportunity: being chosen for special attention that helps you grow your career or showcase your talents.

Invitation. Advancement might mean an invitation: being selected to join a committee or team that has relevance to the CEO or the future of the company.

Mobility. Advancement might mean actually *moving:* heading to Europe or Asia or South America to lead a global initiative—or moving to a different part of the company to take on an exciting challenge.

Visibility. Advancement might mean achieving greater visibility and reputation.

Credibility. Advancement might mean increasing your credibility or building your resume.

Publicity. Advancement might mean receiving an award, publicity, or some other kind of public recognition.

These are just a few examples I've seen springboard leaders into a new level of performance and respect—and yes, promotion—in their careers. What about you?

I ask this question not because I want to discourage you from seeking that next big promotion. On the contrary, expanding your sights to a broader definition of advancement will open up new ideas about how you can get that promotion rather than waiting around, hoping for your turn.

What Will Determine the Result?

Once you're clear on what moving up means to you, you're ready for the next question, which is: what will determine the result? To put it another way, advancement is an outcome. What are the goals you need to set that will lead to that outcome?

Many leaders have goals for their career—becoming a C-level executive, sitting on the executive committee in an executive vice president or senior vice president role, or attaining the highest level of achievement in their organization. Having clarity about what it will mean to have "made it" can revitalize your commitment to making it happen.

Now, what will *determine* that result? "Becoming the CEO someday" is a hard goal to act on, as it depends on so many other factors outside your control. Assuming everything falls into place, you're going to need to be prepared—and in so preparing, you're more likely to move up.

Perhaps that seems obvious. If you want to reach a big goal, you have to meet the objectives that will lead to the goal. But you'd be surprised how easily people get distracted from what they want—just long enough to get themselves off track. You need perfect alignment in order to advance: a clear sense of exactly what you want and an equally clear understanding of what it takes to get there.

To find the elements of your career that will lead to the result you want, consider the ways you will need to develop yourself and demonstrate your readiness to advance. Some of these elements will be related to the role you want, many of which we touched on in our discussion about performance.

- If you want to be an exemplary people leader, you'll need to master talent management.
- If you want to succeed at the higher executive levels, you'll need to develop strategy and the ability to shape a corporate vision.
- If you want to be the CEO, you're likely to need financial acumen and stellar communication skills.

Some of the elements will be related to the behind-the-scenes work of personal leadership, which include the very topics we've discussed in this book.

- Expanding and leveraging your network.
- Establishing strong relationships with your mentors and sponsors.
- Refining your executive presence.
- Overachieving in your performance.
- Getting recognized as a stand-out among your peers.

Take a moment to think about what specific areas you will need to focus on in order to move up in the way you have in mind. What will be the drivers of those results?

What Else Matters to You?

Sometimes we can get so locked in on a goal that the rest of the world goes away. Apart from the singularly focused and the ultra-ambitious, most of us have other things that also matter in our lives. Even when we have big career objectives like moving up into that next level position, we find our happiness when we balance them with our intentions for our personal lives, like staying healthy and being with family.

Revisit Claire Shipman and Katty Kay's description of the "New All" at the beginning of this chapter. How would you write a New All for yourself? What would you include?

NEGOTIATION CHECKLIST

To gain advancement in your career—however you define it—you're going to have to *ask*. Women stereotypically claim to dislike negotiating or not to do it well, but in reality women have the strengths and skills to be exceptional negotiators.

Selena Rezvani, author of *Pushback: How Smart Women Ask and Stand Up for What They Want,* has some pointers to help you negotiate your next big move.[5] Here's a checklist based on Rezvani's work you can use to get prepared.

_____ I know what I want to ask for.

_____ I know what's at stake if I don't ask.

_____ I know where I am ready to take a stand, and I know where I'm flexible.

_____ I believe I deserve to ask for what I want.

_____ I recognize my case is worth pursuing.

_____ I have prepared for negotiating by strengthening my negotiating skills and choosing a positive, productive mindset.

_____ I have talked to others to check my assumptions and gain new perspectives that will help me be successful.

_____ I have done my homework by informing myself with facts and data, considering my counterpart's point of view, and choosing the right time, place, and style for the discussion.

_____ I am genuinely interested in finding a win–win, and I see the negotiation as "us versus the problem" instead of "me versus them."

_____ I have considered the strengths I bring to the task of negotiating to build my confidence.

_____ I have practiced the conversation in a role play, visualized it going well, or both.

_____ I am focused and prepared to engage in the conversation.

_____ I have a plan for following up on the conversation by reflecting on it internally and communicating externally with a summary of our discussion to create clarity and agreement.

The Cost of Not Negotiating

If negotiating isn't your strong suit, Rezvani's strong suggestion is to learn the skill and practice. She points out that the cost of *not* negotiating is far too great. "By omitting negotiation from salary discussions," she writes, "a woman stands to lose more than $1,000,000 over the course of her life compared to a man."[6] At that price, you have a lot to lose. You have much more to gain by advocating on your own behalf.

Q&A with Howard and Joelle

It sounds like what you're saying is the only way to get promoted is to get the very best results, but hey, that may never be enough.

Howard: What I said was that having exceptional performance is the best way to make it difficult for someone not to give you the job. When you are clearly far and away the best candidate, because of your results in every area, it would be hard for a hiring manager to defend a decision not to hire you.

Joelle: But that doesn't mean it couldn't happen. He or she might not hire you.

Howard: Sure.

Joelle: That hardly seems fair.

Howard: Of course. It may not be fair.

I'm not saying if you have the best performance you will always get ahead. I am saying your performance may be the only variable you can control. And by performance, I mean performance in every area. Performance is multi-dimensional. It may include your metrics on revenue, customer retention, perceived value by other peers in the organization, the degree to which you are seen as multi-faceted versus single-faceted. Those are just examples, by the way. That is not a definitive list. There is no definitive list.

That's why, even though I believe you should focus intently on your performance, at some point you have to realize your performance is not the sole determinant of promotion.

Is it so unreasonable to think it would be fairer to have a checklist of things I could use to know I'm on track to get ahead?

Howard: No, it's not unreasonable to think that would be fair. It might be unreasonable to think it's possible, or that it would work.

Joelle: Let me think out loud on that.

I can think of lots of examples in which organizations, leaders, employees, and even coaches (myself included!) have tried to make the list.

- In organizations, we call them competencies. These are the competencies you need to have to do well in your role.
- With executives and employees, they may be strengths and areas of concern, say, in a performance review or an Executive Development Plan. If you focus on improving the things your boss wants you to improve, you can expect to be in good shape.
- In coaching, we call them focus areas or objectives. They are areas on which an individual needs to focus in order to achieve his or her vision and goals.

What you're saying is (I think) these are fine tools for helping people focus their attention on their performance and perhaps to look for milestones that show they're doing well. But they don't guarantee a promotion.

Howard: Yup! Next time look at the successful applicant and see how many competencies they are missing.

How do I choose the right perspective on getting a promotion, so I'm focused and effective (not frustrated or obsessed)?

Joelle: I like the idea of viewing situations not as fair or unfair, but rather choosing a perspective that's going to work for you. I work with executives on this a lot: choosing how to view a situation so you can not only live with it (whatever "it" is), but actually find the motivators and the advantages to the situation and thrive within it.

Howard: There are so many different ways to look at any situation. You always want to find the perspective that gets the best results.

For instance, it's not necessarily helpful to assume that the route to a promotion is fair and then push back when it's not. A more helpful perspective might be to accept that the route may be unfair, and you can still do your best to influence and give yourself the best shot at advancement.

To give another example, it's not that helpful to take things personally and dwell on them forever. If you do, you'll make yourself miserable. Men sometimes seem to let things go more easily than women. Even if something happens that frustrates them, they can let it go. Women sometimes hold on longer than is helpful, and they end up pushing back instead of moving on.

It's also frankly not that helpful to be so focused on promotion. It's so much more rewarding and productive to focus on self-fulfillment and results. I can honestly say from the first time I went into a job in an organization, not once did I ever spend a day worrying about what my next promotion was. Never thought about it, never planned it, I just went and blew the doors off with my performance.

Joelle: I'm definitely a big fan of choosing the right perspective. And for sure I've seen women push back instead of moving on. I'm not sure about the part about not focusing on promotion, though. For me, planning is everything. I've heard many mentors and sponsors of successful women help them plan their career path, and for some women it's their path to fulfillment! That may be a difference of style. However, I do see your point that obsessing on promotion can be detrimental, especially if it keeps you from enjoying and excelling in the role you're in right now.

I once read, "If you are doing everything you can to achieve your goals, you have every right to be optimistic." That, to me, is an assuring balance and a good mantra for people with high aspirations. It holds you accountable while helping you let go of the things you can't control.

It seems to me that at some point all of this effort and focus on performance and promotions leads to a decision, on both sides. Either you get the job or you don't. Either you stay or you leave. Is that the only choice?

Howard: Can you see any other choice? Let's say you feel that way. Your boss says to you, you're the number one performer in our organization. You're great. You ask, do you think I could move up to the next level? Your boss says, yes, I think you could. You've shown performance in this role, and I think you'd be great. Then the first job opens up at the next level. You don't get it. The second job opens up. You don't get it. What do you do?

Joelle: Well, I suppose I have options. Either I love my job and so I stay, or I get mad and I leave. I could look for another opportunity elsewhere in the company. Or I could find out why I didn't get the job, and if there's a reason that's under my control, I can get to work improving on that.

Howard: Right. If you deserved the job and didn't get it, that's a judgment on the organization. If it turns out the other candidate was better, then you can keep working on yourself. Or, has your boss been honest on the things that are holding you back. All of us are not that great at being open and honest with our best performers—we don't want to risk the consequences of honesty.

What if the situation really is unfair?

Joelle: What if you think it is an unfair decision? What if you really are the best performer, have the best results, are clearly the best person for the job, and never get it? What if you suspect it has to do with the fact that you're a woman, or any other form of bias for that matter?

Howard: Sometimes what we think is a gender issue (or a race issue, or a generational issue) is really just an issue. In this case the issue is your performance. Were you the best candidate for the job, or weren't you? Layering in the other issues only complicates the matter.

Joelle: But it is a complicated matter! What if there's discrimination going on?

Howard: There very well could be. That doesn't mean there aren't also other issues.

Let's put it this way. Assume for the moment you're a highly talented executive woman. You feel you have reached the highest level you can in the organization, and you get positive feedback all around. You have every reason to expect that you should be promoted, and you never are. Worse, when it does look like you got a promotion to the seat you want, the job gets leveled down and now you just have more responsibility without the title, compensation or salary.

A man gets the job in a new position that has been created at a higher level with all three of things, and you cry foul. This certainly looks like the glass ceiling.

Joelle: I see it all the time.

Howard: Okay. So what do you do? We already identified the four options: you stay, you leave, you look elsewhere in the company, or you work on yourself. The choices are still the same.

Joelle: It sounds like you're saying that's okay, then. Even if it's gender bias, you can't do anything about it anyway, so why try?

Howard: I'm just saying don't give the gender issue more power than it deserves. It may be about gender, but you are still the one to choose how you will handle it. What options do you have? Are you going to make a big fuss about the gender bias, accuse your boss of something you can't prove, and create a reputation for yourself you might not want? Are you going to sue? Do you think that will help you move up?

And even if it does, how happy are you going to be? If you get promoted under duress by this chauvinist boss of yours, is that going to work out well in the end? Is he suddenly going to get an epiphany and give you more opportunities in the future? I doubt it!

Joelle: I think there are a lot of people out there who would say you should make a fuss, that you should call attention to discrimination when you see it, and that the person who should have to change is the one who's in the wrong.

I guess what I hear you saying is, if you believe that as a woman you have no future in this company, and if you see patterns along gender lines that you find unacceptable, any of those responses are your choice. But it doesn't mean those choices would move you up.

I've seen several talented executive women choose to leave their companies. They could see the senior leadership levels were filled with men, and they left. They voted with their feet. Women seem to be doing this more and more. They're choosing not to work for companies that don't show evidence of promoting women to the top. I suppose the same is true for choosing not to work for bosses who don't promote women, either.

Howard: If you are applying for a job for a boss or organization that appears to discriminate based on race or gender, ask yourself the question—"How much do I want to work here?" Supply and demand will always take care of these bad organizations and leaders. It comes down to how much you want to fight.

And, at the same time, be sure you're not using gender as an excuse. Sometimes there really is an underlying issue related to performance, or a number of other reasons why you might not move up.

Heidi and Jen: The End of the Story

Heidi and Jen were frustrated at the disconnect between their visions for their lives and careers and their bosses' perspective. One of them couldn't seem to get the promotion she wanted, and the other was being ushered toward one she didn't want.

They decided they needed a new approach.

First they helped each other get clear and articulate about what they wanted, and then they committed to communicating it with their managers.

Heidi had to go back to her boss and share—with no anger or resentment—that she was disappointed by the missed opportunity and wanted to learn what it would take to get ahead. It led to a humbling but meaningful conversation that helped Heidi better prepare for the next career opportunity and renewed her motivation to strive.

Jen had to meet with her boss and let him know she wanted to keep her job in sales. She made the case that she was still worth the time and investment, and conveyed her intention to be in the top 3 percent of sales producers instead of moving into management—an approach that benefitted the company, made great use of her talents, and fit with her lifestyle.

Heidi and Jen's conversations changed their managers' perspectives about what "success" can be and gave them confidence that as they continued to excel in their careers, they would also continue to advance.

Key Points

1. Advancement primarily means being promoted, especially at the top of the organization and above the infamous line where women's careers tend to stop. It can also mean moving successfully into a new phase in your career, which may or may not include the traditional corporate image of promotion.
2. The questions about advancement for women in leadership are multiple and complex.
3. With a newly empowered perspective about what success and achievement mean to you, you will finally understand what women mean when they say they have it all. You just may have it all, too.
4. Leaders and their managers often make assumptions about advancement, and that can lead to a dissatisfying situation on both sides.
5. You need perfect alignment in order to advance: a clear sense of exactly what you want and an equally clear understanding of what it takes to get there.

Questions for Reflection

1. What does advancement mean to you now?
2. What could you do now to prepare for the opportunities you want?
3. Do a critical self-assessment. Is there (truthfully, now) anything about which you are complaining, without doing something positive to change it? If you are, can you actually change it? If you can, are you doing it? If you can't, can you move on and find a more positive way to make an impact?
4. What fulfills you in your current role? How can you make the most of the situation you're in right now? Or what changes do you need to make to get that sense of fulfillment?

CHAPTER 8

The Feedback Advantage (How do you know how you're *really* doing?)

"By interpreting the 'mirror' of our behavior and habits at very close range, we have the unique opportunity for objectivity, and dramatically enhanced performance."
—Saly Glassman, Managing Director-Wealth Management, Merrill Lynch Bank of America

Holly

Holly had a lot to be proud of, or so she thought. She had been the most senior woman at one of the hottest tech firms in Silicon Valley. In fact, she was the only woman in the top 100 executives. She received plum assignments from her boss, the CEO. She was extremely autonomous in her role and had all the power she needed to get things done. Imagine her surprise when her peer-evaluated performance review showed her receiving the lowest score possible.

"It affected my compensation. It affected my standing. It took me down in the eyes of my team," Holly complained. "When I asked my boss about the feedback, he just blew it off like it didn't mean anything. 'If you're concerned about it, go talk to Rachael,' he said. She's the VP of HR."

Holly did go talk to Rachael, who gave her the feedback she knew as best she could. From her understanding, Holly needed to be a better team player, focus more on developing her team, and adopt a less demanding demeanor. Fairly vague feedback, but when Holly pressed for detail, her manager didn't have much to add. Holly had never heard any of this before and found the very notion of the feedback offensive. Should she really start changing her approach when to date her leadership style seemed to work so well? What credence could she give to the VP of HR? Shouldn't she rather listen to her boss? But how could she take her boss's advice and brush off the feedback, when all of the rewards of her role were tied to her evaluation? To Holly, none of this made any sense. Caught between resentment and confusion, Holly failed to get further specifics on the feedback and made no visible changes in her approach to leadership.

The next year when the peer review process rolled around again, Holly was a basket of nerves. She got the worst score for a second year in a row. A week later, she lost her job. She never saw it coming.

Feedback in any setting has the potential to be constructive—a roadmap leaders can follow to discover where to focus their learning.

So what does one do with a story like Holly's? In her case, we see how feedback can backfire. Some people get feedback but it doesn't help. Some people don't get feedback they need. That's *not* how feedback should work. Feedback should be a source of information and growth.

You will gain so much more out of the feedback available to you when you see it from every angle—how it can help, how it can hurt, how to get what you need, how to avoid being blindsided, and, hopefully, how to use feedback as a means of improving yourself on an ongoing basis.

Feedback is an essential part of your development—a positive, worthwhile investment that pays off by helping you succeed at every stage of your career. In this chapter, we help you get it.

The Feedback Dilemma

Feedback is the ongoing formal and informal input you get from the sources all around you. It includes the explicit messages you get from the people with whom you work, but feedback can also come from your own observations, the way others react to you, and your results.

Where feedback gets troublesome is when it's absent, misleading, incomplete, or poorly received.

That happens far more than we'd like, which is why so many organizations are revisiting their performance review processes and trying to get it right. Meanwhile, feedback remains treacherous for women. The Center for Talent Innovation reports:

- Women are 32 percent less likely to receive any feedback from male superiors.[1]
- When they do get feedback, 81 percent of women say they have trouble responding to it, because it's so "distressingly contradictory."[2]

- When women make up less than 25 percent of an applicant pool, they are more likely to be negatively evaluated.[3]

In addition, we have observed at the Leadership Research Institute that compared to men:

- Women tend to be harder on themselves when receiving feedback from others.
- Women are also hard on themselves when they *self*-assess, tending to underrate their own abilities.
- Women can feel overwhelmed or crushed by feedback.
- Women tend to get softer feedback from others—despite the fact that rigorous feedback is one of the ways leaders strengthen their capabilities.

In other words, more so for women than for men, feedback—meant to be a helpful vehicle to move leaders forward through self-improvement—can be a minefield.

Resolving this dilemma means prioritizing feedback while putting it in perspective and learning to handle it effectively. You'll find the balance by taking the feedback *seriously* without taking it *personally*. That means finding the most valuable messages, letting go the rest, and focusing your attention on improving where it counts.

Trying to succeed without useful feedback is like driving at night with the headlights off. It can be done, but we wouldn't advise it. In contrast, if you fuel yourself with a steady stream of information about what's working, what's not working, and what you need to change, you will be able to keep yourself moving forward on the road to success.

The Feedback Advantage

The feedback advantage puts you on the inside track. Suddenly success isn't a mystery anymore. You can get the truth about what you need to succeed and take action on it for the best results.

At the Leadership Research Institute, we see feedback as a cornerstone to effective leadership. We provide employee engagement surveys to more than 100 organizations. We provide survey-based and interview-based feedback to leaders at every level, from CEOs of Fortune 500 companies to entry-level employees, all around the world. Our research, which includes more than four and a half million data points gathered from hundreds of companies over the course of several decades, points to a strong conclusion:

The number one predictor of leadership effectiveness is a commitment to self-improvement.

That means that out of everything you could do to improve your career, showing yourself to be devoted to your own growth and learning will do more to establish your success as a leader than anything else. The executives we interviewed agreed. Rose Marcario, CEO of Patagonia, put it this way. "The more committed you are to working on yourself, the more you bring to your work."

You may not be able to do much about the culture of feedback in your organization company wide. Feedback as it exists in organizational life is problematic. Systems are flawed; processes are imperfect, but it's a mistake to think it's out of your control.

You *have* control over your ability to get good feedback. You can educate yourself about how good feedback should work and take the initiative to get it for yourself. Whether your company has good feedback structures or not, you can take advantage of the wealth of information available through feedback—both positive and negative—that will boost your confidence and the constructive criticism that can save or propel your career.

You have a variety of options for feedback.

An Interview-Based 360-Degree Profile

The gold standard in feedback is a thorough, interview-based 360-degree profile. More customized and personal than most assessments, this kind of feedback involves asking for input on your effectiveness from the people all around you—your manager, your direct reports, and your peers. A consultant or executive coach designs the questions with you (and perhaps your manager), then conducts the interviews. At the end, you receive a customized report of the results. The information you receive is portrait of you as a leader. It's the safest, most complete and confidential way for women to get honest feedback.

Susan Clarke was the president of Accident and Health for North America at AIG. She described the effect her interview-based 360 had on her.

What's unique about an interview-based 360 is that it is so rich with information. It gave me a descriptive account of who I am and how I come across. Everything was clear and in-depth. The information was invaluable.

With her 360, Clarke was able to understand not just what feedback her coworkers had for her, but specifically also (and with examples) how she was leading that was effective as well as where she could make changes for an even better impact.

This kind of 360 is most beneficial when you are either preparing for or have recently received a promotion, or when you are running into struggles with your leadership results, as it will give you the clearest, most specific, actionable feedback you can get.

Survey-Based 360 Feedback

An equally valuable (and often less expensive) alternative to an interview-based 360 is a survey-based 360. Again, feedback is gathered on your behalf from a variety of important stakeholders in your career, only this time through a form, or more likely, an online survey. The benefit of this kind of 360 is that it's more anonymous than an interview-based 360, and taking advantages of economies of scale, it can also incorporate feedback from a much larger number of people very easily.

It's helpful for women to have a wide variety of perspectives, which avoids the danger of getting derailed by one person's feedback. If the interview-based 360 is about depth, the survey-based 360 is about breadth.

Self-Assessments

Self-assessments are research-based quizzes that reveal your attributes. Each assessment will yield different information. You can take assessments to discover

- personality traits,
- leadership style,
- behaviors,
- thinking preferences,
- natural strengths,
- career derailers, and
- the roles in which you'll be happiest in life.

Such assessments reveal information you might not come up with on your own, giving you fresh, new insight into the characteristics that define you as a leader.

The particular value of self-assessments for women is the way they strengthen your sense of self. That's important for women to have in place, as it grounds them and helps them sort through conflicting messages they may receive about what they "should" be to be seen as an effective leader. The combination of good data from self-assessments and quality feedback from others gives women the opportunity to make their own determination about what works.

Interactive Performance Reviews

Any kind of performance review is designed to give you feedback. Many companies are moving away from traditional performance reviews to an ongoing checking-in process between managers and their employees, so that your feedback becomes part of an interactive dialogue. Even if your company doesn't offer this, you can structure the conversation yourself. Later in this chapter we show you how. It's critical for women to lead this conversation, given the research that shows they may not get the feedback otherwise.

Reflective Questions

Another form of self-assessment is ongoing reflection. All you need to succeed with this approach is three simple questions:

1. What's working?
2. What's not working?
3. What do I need to change?

Ask these questions often and pose them to other people, and you'll have an ongoing gauge as to how you're doing and where to focus your attention.

As we mentioned at the beginning of this chapter, your commitment to self-improvement raises your credibility as a leader. Engaging others in your reflection communicates that commitment. It's also an efficient way to get a clear direction on how to be the best leader you can be.

In all of these ways, you can access the feedback you need. Your job is to request feedback when it's missing and receive it well when it's provided. You'll not only learn what you need to do but you'll also communicate that you are a learner, which in turn will enhance your reputation as a leader.

MARSHALL GOLDSMITH ON FEEDBACK

The foremost expert on feedback is Marshall Goldsmith. Goldsmith has published more than 30 books and is recognized as the world's foremost thought leader in the field of leadership. In his book, *What Got You Here Won't Get You There*,[4] he simplifies the process of getting feedback to a simple question: "How can I do better?"

If all you do is make a habit of asking people you respect, again and again, "How can I do better?" you'll have plenty of feedback to keep you busy.

The Benefits of Feedback

When you receive feedback and are seen to be acting on that feedback, your stock goes up in the eyes of others.

Feedback is essential for developing your self-awareness, and without self-awareness, how will you know where to direct your efforts at self-improvement? With ongoing feedback, you gain:

- A clear sense of what you're doing that works.
- Specificity about where and how to improve.
- Clarity about others' expectations of you.
- A gauge for measuring your ongoing performance.
- Perspective from others about what it's like to work with you.
- Evidence you can use to support your efforts to advance in your career.
- The opportunity to show yourself to be a credible, dedicated leader who cares about being as effective as possible.

More than that, if done well, the process of eliciting feedback, and then learning from it and following through, can be one through which you develop rich, strong relationships with important people in your professional life:

- Your manager.
- Your peers.
- Your direct reports.
- Your customers or clients.
- Your mentors and sponsors.
- Your network.

The best part of all is that feedback is all around you, and it's yours for the asking.

Our Perspectives

Howard

People fall into a number of pitfalls when it comes to feedback. They take it too personally. They get defensive. They rationalize it and reject it. None of this is helpful.

Your willingness to listen, learn, and improve will do more for your perception as a committed leader than anything else. A few simple steps on your part, in addition to getting the feedback, will make the process pay off.

Bring an Open Mind

A common response to feedback is defensiveness. When we do surveys at the Leadership Research Institute, we often ask participants providing feedback to rate the recipient on their willingness to receive the feedback and make a change. This kind of awareness can help a leader remember that improvement following feedback is an expectation—and you can't meet that expectation if you dismiss everything you hear.

The worst case scenario occurs when feedback shuts you down. When you shut down, you don't take in the feedback at all. Now you are not only ignoring what you might need to change or improve but you are also closing off all possibilities of getting the insights you need to learn to do things differently.

Before you discount any kind of feedback, at least make the effort to understand it and either validate or invalidate it.

Treat Feedback as Feedback

Feedback is just information. Feedback isn't the gospel truth. Feedback is someone's opinion of you, wrapped in their personal experiences, biases, and observations. Some of it is valuable and some of it isn't.

You can ignore feedback or you can accept it. If you accept it, don't grumble about it. If you don't, let it go. If you let it go and it comes back again later, at that point you'd better get serious about making changes.

When I coach somebody, I assume when they read their feedback that they haven't gotten this information before. When I think of all the executives I've known over the years who have been fired, the most common reaction I've heard is, "I didn't even know this was coming." There was a time I didn't believe them when they said that. Now I realize it's sometimes true. Sometimes leaders haven't received the feedback before, or if they have, they haven't heard it, which equates to the same thing.

But from the moment they get their feedback . . . now they know. Their job is to judge the feedback for themselves and decide how accurate it is. Once you know the issues, you need to address them. Apply the feedback and reassess your progress every few months to see how it's making an impact.

Follow Through

It's not just receiving the feedback that's important. Once you have the feedback, you have do actually do something with it, including reflecting on the results, creating a plan of action based on the information, and following through with the people who gave you the feedback.

We at the Leadership Research Institute have specific suggestions for what to do.

1. **Thank your participants.** Thank your responders for providing the feedback, and let them know what you've learned from it.
2. **Share what you've learned.** Share what pleased you to hear in the feedback and what two or three areas you've discovered need improvement.
3. **Describe what you'll do now.** Identify the top priorities you'll be focusing on in your action plan. As you do, "link and label:" connect what you heard in the feedback to the actions you'll be taking. This gives change efforts visibility, so others will be able to see what you're doing to improve the impact it's having on your effectiveness.
4. **Ask for further suggestions.** Invite the people who gave you feedback initially to give you any additional information that will help you be successful in implementing the changes you want to make.
5. **Follow up periodically.** Reiterate the key messages you've received, provide an update on the steps you've taken to improve, and emphasize your commitment to continue the learning.[5]

Taking these steps will communicate to everyone around you that you are a person who listens and learns and who wants to be your best. Again, the number one predictor of perceived effectiveness is your commitment to your own self-improvement. It's only part of the process to *be* committed. You need to *show* you're committed.

Otherwise, no one will know. If they don't know you've received the feedback, what would make them think it was worth giving it to you in the first place?

Joelle

At the beginning of this chapter, we shared Holly's experience with feedback. She couldn't make sense of the feedback she got and couldn't respond to it, and she was ultimately fired. Her story is probably the worst I've ever heard when it comes to feedback. She was shocked and devastated. We can learn from her how to get feedback that will lead to a more positive experience.

Feedback in Full (At First)

I always recommend considering all of the feedback you receive in full . . . at first. Keep your defenses down and listen to what's being offered.

The feedback Holly got from her 360 was painful—the lowest possible score on her peer review. The feedback she got from HR was even more so—three vague explanations about what "might have been" the reason for her score. But the worst feedback of all was the feedback she got from her boss: "Don't worry about it. It's probably nothing."

Holly took his advice. As a consequence, she ultimately got fired. Why? Partly because her boss wasn't leading the peer review process; he was only one voice on a committee of Holly's peers who were weighing in on her performance. Perhaps she was performing on the measures that most affected him, but she was failing in the eyes of her peers. The other reason she was mistaken to ignore the feedback was that she wasn't reading her boss's signals. In sending her to talk to the VP of HR, he was intending to communicate indirectly that there were some tough messages she needed to hear, and that the VP of HR would be the best person to give her the message. For whatever reason, he didn't give her the really tough feedback directly; he gave her the softer, watered-down version. Holly could have dug a little deeper to get at the truth.

What lesson does Holly's experience hold for other women who want to avoid her fate? Listen to the feedback. Feedback is often tough. It can be downright humiliating. It can be confusing, contradictory, and it can blow your self-confidence, if you let it.

Look more closely. If you put your defenses down, could there be something to learn? Holly was so deeply offended and stunned by the feedback that she couldn't get to a state of openness and readiness to learn. If she had, it's possible she would have stretched herself to try new leadership styles. Perhaps the outcome would have been different if she was open to change.

For the record, I don't think any of this is exclusive to women. Plenty of men I've coached have been defensive about feedback and rejected the news they needed to hear. One reaction to feedback that never helps is denial.

Piece by Piece

After weighing all the feedback, go through it piece by piece and ask yourself:

- What's worth keeping?
- What's helpful to me now?

This is especially important if the feedback is hard for you to receive.

Once you've pulled out the pieces of the feedback you want to focus on now, build an action plan. Choose one or two themes and determine what you want to do with it. Do you need more information? Do you want to learn more about how to improve? Are there steps you need to take? Behaviors you need to change? Make a plan to work on the areas of greatest impact, and the feedback will be doing its job.

As for the rest, you can let it go . . . for now. Save it somewhere, so you can find it if it becomes relevant again. Then go back to focusing on being your best as a leader.

Gender Bias and Gender Barriers

One piece of Holly's story I do question is whether her boss was being honest when he said the feedback meant "nothing." Maybe he simply couldn't bring himself to give her the hard truth. Perhaps it was because she was a friend; perhaps it was because she was a woman; perhaps it had nothing to do with either of those reasons, but in the end, he avoided the issue. Someone else could explain.

Naturally, Holly would have been better served if her boss had been able to provide the feedback himself. But before we write him off, it's worth considering the position men are in. In the same way that men find it difficult to comment on a woman's dress, manner, and attitude, perhaps he found it too risky to comment on her personality. Men have been sued for less.

It's not clear what Holly's boss really meant when he sent her to Rachael for more information. The lack of transparency in the process is worrisome. You may never know whether you're getting the real story, but you can shore up your chances for good information if you go to a variety of sources, include both men and women, and make it clear you're open to the message. Earlier in this chapter, we gave you a variety of ways to get feedback, such as 360-degree profiles and self-assessments. All of these are great options, and any one of them is better than the kind of feedback Holly got, which was verbal second-hand information, delivered vaguely.

Also, while it's possible Holly had some serious hurdles to clear to raise her peer review scores, it's equally possible she was a victim of the process. Rumors circulated at the time that in this forced-ranking process, she was the only woman being evaluated. None of the men would give their guys the lowest score, and someone had to get it, so they gave it to Holly. Maybe since she was the CEO's longtime friend they thought she was safe.

Without being in the room, there's no way to know, and in this case, it wouldn't be fair to judge the men giving the feedback—or Holly herself, or her boss, or even Rachael. And that's the downside to feedback. How do you know what's real?

I'm not suggesting Holly's feedback wasn't fair or that the men in her company discriminated against her. I do think all of the players in a setting like this need to be aware of where gender *could* play a part in evaluation and the effect a poor process could have on everyone involved.

Either way, what do you do if you sense bias in the system? The same questions that can help you discern what feedback to keep and what to toss can be helpful in addressing any unfairness you detect in the process.

- What battles will you fight?
- What can you let go?
- Where do you need to watch and see?

Perhaps the best approach would be to accept the possibility of unfairness, but never let it be an excuse and refuse to play the victim. Weigh the feedback as carefully as you would in any situation, take from it what's worth taking, and leave the rest behind.

Getting away from Holly for a moment and back to you, there's one important message every leader should hear. Data speak. The more data you can get, from the widest variety of sources and the most important people around you, the better you'll know yourself. The more you know yourself, the more accurately you can judge where you need to improve and where you can be confident you're doing well. Bias can be a part of any feedback process. If you do encounter a hint of bias—as unconscious as it may be—you'll have the data to give you an accurate picture of your strengths and challenges as a leader.

The Role of Executive Coaching

One-on-one coaching provides a place to work out challenges of the feedback process, so it all goes well.

Through coaching you gain clarity, perspectives, and direction that come from interacting with someone who cares as much about your success as you do. Almost no one else in your life can provide the kind of confidential, informed, objective, and productive learning environment you will experience with your executive coach.

This is especially true when it comes to feedback. Women have been shown to be more self-critical than men, and as a result, feedback can hit us pretty hard. You may have developed a thick skin in your years in business, and perhaps you no longer feel the sting that can accompany feedback, but many women struggle with feedback—both the criticism *and* the praise.

Your experience receiving feedback—especially large-scale, multirater feedback—will be greatly enhanced by working with your coach, whether your coach is an external executive coach, an internal coach, or your manager. Your coach will help you as follows:

- Discern the most salient feedback.
- Process the feedback to make sense of it.
- Determine the most effective action steps.
- Successfully implement the follow-up process.
- Make the changes to improve your effectiveness (as well as your scores).
- Communicate the positive changes you've made so you become recognized as a leader who is increasing your impact.

For executive women, the importance of executive coaching goes well beyond feedback. In fact, the *lack* of coaching actually *hampers* female executives, and inadequate career development has kept women from reaching the top ranks of the corporate ladder.[6] Give yourself the opportunity to work through your feedback with your coach as a partner, and you will make the most of the feedback process and the results.

Q&A with Howard and Joelle

What if you're not getting any feedback?

Joelle: We say your willingness to listen, learn, and improve will do more for your perception as a committed leader than anything else, but that assumes you're getting the feedback. What if you're not getting the feedback? Holly, who we talked about at the beginning of this chapter, never got the actionable, specific feedback she needed until it was too late. Other executives we know who were fired didn't have clarification on the feedback either. It's not that they didn't accept it. They never actually received it.

Howard: There are two ways to look at that. One is, they did too have the feedback. Holly got the feedback from the performance review. The executives got the feedback when they lost their jobs. The process of responding to the feedback begins the minute the feedback comes in.

The other way of looking at it is that the feedback is already available. You may have to go out and get it if it doesn't come to you!

Joelle: So you're saying people should ask for feedback.

Howard: Yes! The more you know about yourself, the better off you are. You can always throw out the parts that don't mean much. The rest will show you exactly where you're good and where you can build on your strengths, or where you have room to grow and improve. What could be more valuable than that?

Joelle: In my observation, a whole lot of people are terrible at giving feedback. They avoid it, sugar coat it or minimize it rather than deal with a touchy situation head-on. This is why I so strongly advocate going out and getting your own feedback. So your boss doesn't give you good feedback? Ask for it specifically. Still don't get it? Ask someone else—another manager you work with, a peer, a team member. Keep asking and asking. Knowledge is power. Even though I understand that, for many reasons, a male boss may not give his female direct report the tough feedback she needs to hear, that doesn't mean she can't get it at all. It just means she hasn't gotten it from him.

The feedback is out there. It's up to you to be sure you're gathering it up for yourself and making the most of what it has to offer.

What if you don't agree with the feedback?

Joelle: Sometimes people take feedback too personally, get defensive, or dismiss it. But what if the feedback actually isn't valid? Are you supposed to take everything you hear as true and useful?

Howard: Not at all. You should take from the feedback the valuable information it contains and align it to what you're trying to achieve. Where's your best opportunity? Where's your worst liability? How do you maximize one and minimize the other?

What you can't do is ask for feedback and then argue against it once you've gotten it. If that's your intention you're better off not asking for the feedback at all. When you ask for feedback, you raise expectations. You're communicating to people that you care about what they have to say and want to use it to improve for the better. They get a very hopeful, optimistic view of you, which you've earned by taking the initiative to learn more about yourself. That's all good.

What happens if after all that goodwill you throw the feedback out without so much as a moment's consideration? What do you suppose will be the impact then?

Your ability to accept and receive feedback gracefully is important whether or not you agree with everything it says. Treat people with respect, and give their input consideration. Then you have a choice as to how you respond and choose to change.

Joelle: Even if you don't agree with the feedback, don't fight it. Say, "Thank you," and mean it. If every time you get feedback you start explaining yourself (why this or that happened or didn't happen, why this or that is true or not true), people will feel neglected in their efforts to help you, and they won't give you feedback again.

Holly: The End of the Story

Holly believed she had been a victim of a mishandled performance review process. After she was fired from her company—an outcome she attributed to the feedback—Holly retired for good. It was a dispiriting end to a long career.

But there are other examples where feedback is working.

Kelly was a new member of the leadership team at a thrilling new start-up that was growing at an exhilarating pace. The speed of progress and the pace of change were dizzying, and Kelly was racing to keep up. Time and again, she hit bumps in her new role, but her manager kept shoring her up, giving her feedback, and guiding her with ideas and counsel. He had hired a consulting team to bring a development process to the company, including 360-degree feedback for all managers at her level, several self-assessment instruments, and individual executive development plans. It was a wealth of information, and Kelly soaked it all in.

She also went above and beyond, using feedback as her headlights and her guardrails as to whether she was staying on track to her goals. She kept an open mind as she gathered as much feedback as she could. She used wisdom and discernment to make sense of the feedback, pulling out the most helpful and relevant messages. As a result, she developed a reputation with her manager of being a learner and a leader—one the company would continue to invest in for years to come.

Meanwhile, back at Holly's company, the learning was far from over.

Holly's experience became one of many examples that started surfacing in the company in which talented leaders were given poor performance review scores with little (if any) clear feedback or evidence. Reliable, well-performing employees were getting low marks in the system, and those marks affected their promotability and their paychecks. Accountability was lacking and the perception was that the more powerful voices in the room would act in their own best interests to the detriment of everyone else. The lack of transparency in the process was challenged by leaders and managers who wanted a fairer system. When the complaints reached a critical mass, something finally had to be done.

It took a couple of years, but eventually the old performance review system was taken out and replaced with a more equitable and transparent model. Now, instead of relying on committees to rank employees against each other, the company teaches leaders and managers how to give clear, direct feedback, supported by evidence. The hope is the company will become a place of learning, where employees at every level commit to understanding where they're strong and where they can improve, and fortunately none of it remains a secret.

Key Points

1. Feedback includes the explicit messages you get from the people with whom you work, but feedback can also come from your own observations, the way others react to you, and your results.
2. Where feedback gets troublesome is when it's absent, misleading, incomplete, or poorly received.
3. Out of everything you could do to improve your career, showing yourself to be devoted to your own growth and learning will do more to establish your success as a leader than anything else.
4. Feedback as it exists in organizational life is problematic. Systems are flawed; processes are imperfect.
5. Whether your company has good feedback structures or not, you can take advantage of the wealth of information available through feedback—both positive and negative—that will boost your confidence and the constructive criticism that can save or propel your career.

Questions for Reflection

1. What are all of the ways you have received feedback over the years? What does it say?
2. Where do you know you're good?
3. Where are your challenges?
4. Where do you need to know more?
5. Who can tell you what you need to hear?
6. How will you stay open to the feedback?
7. What feedback do you need to let go?

CHAPTER 9

The Awareness Advantage
(How can you break through the bias?)

"You have to have personal courage."

—Coretha Rushing, Chief Human
Resources Officer, Equifax

Tamara

Tamara was the EVP at a large investment bank. She was asked to join a council considering how to advance women in a field largely dominated by men. The bank had few women in senior leadership, despite a fairly large pool of talented women in the vice president levels and below.

After the first meeting, Tamara met with her mastermind group— a small group of executive women who met once a month with their coach for group coaching, discussion, and support in achieving their goals.

"Well, how did it go?" her colleagues asked Tamara. She reported, "To his credit, a man initiated the discussion. We were all talking about how to improve the representation of women in management and what the benefits of that would be. The executive facilitating the discussion said, 'We need more balance, more diversity—for decision making purposes. Let's say parity is the goal in ten years.'

"A guy on the other end of the table said, 'Why do we think parity should be the goal?'

*"I didn't know which part offended me more—that it wasn't clear why
we should achieve parity or that the deadline for the goal was ten years
away.*

*"The conversation spiraled down from there. 'What makes us think
women even want to be in management?' one executive posited. 'The
woman who works for me has been in her role for twenty years, and she's
happy in the job she's in.'*

*"Other men at the table agreed, and one even suggested the women
would probably be happier if they had to work less anyway so they could
stay home more with their kids.*

*"In all of this, the head of HR said nothing. He called me afterwards
and congratulated me for staying quiet."*

Tamara's report is only one of many we've heard on bias against
women. Others are far uglier, from abuses of power to sexual assaults to
bosses who get drunk and start handing out favors. Forget the old boys'
club, it's a locker room out there in some of the most prestigious corporate offices you can find.

Of course it's not everywhere. We've spent dozens of years working
in hundreds of companies, and most cultures are based on mutual
respect and professionalism. Hopefully you have been met with only
the best kind of interactions with both men and women throughout
your career.

But we'd be remiss if we ignored what we hear all too often—whether
it's blatant discrimination or subtle biases—in a book dedicated to the
success of leading women. As Thomson and Graham put it in *A Woman's
Place Is in the Boardroom,* "for a bias to be remediable, it must first
become discussable."[1] In this chapter, we're going to discuss it.

The Awareness Dilemma

When we set out to write this book, we made an agreement. We were
going to focus on being helpful to both men and women in identifying the
dilemmas women face, to see whether we could help pave the way to success. We weren't going to bash men on the extreme end of the spectrum
for discriminating against women. We weren't going to blame women on
the other extreme for being part of the problem. We wanted to talk to the
middle—men and women like you, who are committed to a diverse and
effective work environment for talented leaders, who through their efforts
make a positive difference in business.

We're still committed to that vision, but we need to examine the biases
that exist. Overcoming them is a key part of the solution.

- Sexual harassment affects the lives of 40 to 60 percent of working women.
- Less than 1 percent of complaints are false.
- Studies have found that victims of sexual harassment vary in physical appearance, type of dress, age, and behavior. The only thing they have in common is that more than 99 percent of them are women.[2]

Women are affected by bias at every level of an organization. They may not always recognize it, address it, or respond to it appropriately, and but they can be stopped by it and feel powerless to change it. So they are affected, sometimes in very serious ways.

As a result, in addition to the psychological reactions to sexual harassment (depression, anxiety, anger, powerlessness, and guilt) and the physiological reactions (headaches, sleep disturbances, and nightmares), the career-related effects can hinder women at work. They include:

- Decreased job satisfaction.
- Unfavorable performance evaluations.
- Loss of job or promotion.
- Drop in performance due to stress.
- Absenteeism.
- Withdrawal from work.
- Change in career goals.

It's not just women who are affected. Their companies are hurt, too.

In addition to the ethical responsibility of addressing discrimination and protecting employees from harm, corporate leaders have every reason to ensure bias doesn't hurt the business. Discrimination has been shown to contribute to

- poor communication between staff,
- faulty decision making,
- reduced productivity,
- decreased organizational citizenship behavior,
- reduced employee commitment,
- depleted motivation, and
- increased turnover.

Considering all of the above, not to mention the billions of dollars companies invest in leadership programs and initiatives for women that can be undone by bias, the cost of allowing discrimination to continue is too high a price to pay.

One executive we've worked with, a chief human resources officer in the entertainment industry, has become a champion for women in her company. She feels strongly that business leaders need to address discrimination of all kinds.

> I do think you should talk about these things. They should be published. As a chief HR officer, I've seen women intentionally and unintentionally left out of important discussions, ignored for promotions for which they were highly qualified, and insulted by crass, inappropriate behavior. Very senior people are involved, and they should be held accountable. Most women won't say something about their bosses' bad behavior, because they want to work.
>
> These stories need to be out there. They are contemporary and current and they're not going away. They're on Wall Street, they're in Silicon Valley, and they're not isolated events. We need to address them. We're not going to see change until we do.
>
> And it can't just be the women who are complaining. Corporate boards need to start holding executive teams accountable. They know these stories, and they need to not grant the pay packages while ignoring egregious behavior. They need to not allow the situation to continue, however they get it done. They can choose their own remedy—a training remedy, a sourcing remedy, or a courtroom remedy—otherwise, the problem is not going to be solved. Someone inside the club needs to say this is unacceptable.

Our goal in including this chapter is to raise awareness that these negative forces do still exist and perhaps, in so doing, encourage the creation of a safer, more balanced, universally positive culture in every environment where women work.

Resolving this dilemma is going to take far more than a chapter in a book. We can offer some suggestions, but removing the barriers—from the imbalanced makeup of executive boards to the unfortunate actions of individual outliers—is going to require a critical mass of people (both men and women) who are willing to put in the effort. Only then will we create a culture that has zero tolerance for discrimination in all its forms.

Three Categories of Bias

Instances of discrimination run along a continuum, from the subtle to the extreme. We can divide these into at least three categories:

- Institutionalized bias.
- Stealth discrimination.
- Bad behavior.

Sometimes innocently, sometimes silently, and sometimes crudely, corporate settings and the people who work there perpetuate patterns that hold women back.

Institutionalized Bias

Institutionalized bias is defined as the ways in which policies, practices, behaviors, traditions, and structures, although seemingly benign, favor one advantaged group over others. It is not personal. It is not intentional. It is inherent in the design or evolution of the systems in corporate settings. Many executives genuinely believe their companies are a meritocracy, but if there are no women in leadership positions, then some assumptions need to be tested.

Consider common hiring practices. CEO and board positions often require candidates to have operational experience and to have held C-level positions. It's logical—until you realize that fewer women are likely to have had those experiences, effectively eliminating them from the start.

Other examples include

- job structures that make it difficult for women to get back on a career track after returning from maternity leave,
- inflexible working hours,
- conditions that prevent women from effectively managing child care or family care, and
- performance reviews that measure stereotypically masculine characteristics of leadership.

Companies employing them may not even realize they are stacking the deck toward the kinds of people who would succeed in that kind of practice, policy, or system. Bias is built into the process. On the other hand, the fact that many companies are squirmish about releasing their gender and diversity statistics suggests that they realize a problem exists but are reluctant (at least publicly) to expose it.

The subtlety of institutionalized bias makes it difficult to address. Institutionalized biases hide in plain sight—so much a part of daily life that they go undetected, and because they're undetected, they go unchallenged. Grievous conduct in some of the country's finest academic institutions and frat house behavior in most popular brand companies are surprising and troubling, but the fact that the curtain is being pulled back on these realities indicates a raising of awareness, which is where change begins.

Just because institutionalized bias occurs doesn't mean women are defenseless. Women we've coached have fought for positions they were told they weren't qualified for and gotten them. Many have made successful cases for individual and company-wide policies to accommodate flexible schedules and provide better family leave programs. One particularly feisty executive set up a Pack-n-Play in her office and brought her baby to work every day. Women's individual efforts to combat discrimination do make a difference.

As we discuss the way institutionalized bias turns women away from opportunity, we should also remember that many companies are truly embracing changes that make opportunity available to everyone. To cite a few encouraging examples, several companies have experimented with initiatives that specifically seek to accommodate women through a variety of programs, such as flexible work options, mentoring and professional development programs, "returnships" for working mothers following time off with family, and even partnerships for women who work part-time.[3]

Stealth Discrimination

Slightly more transparent than institutionalized bias is stealth discrimination or paternalistic bias. Stealth discrimination can be defined as a pattern of limiting a person's opportunities based on assumptions that aren't necessarily true.

Karie Willyerd, author of *Workplace 2020: How Innovative Companies Attract, Develop, and Keep Tomorrow's Employees Today*, described it to us this way.

> There are two kinds of discrimination—one is overt; one is covert. It's the second one that's not so obvious. People don't realize how they're getting treated. They just don't get the toughest assignments. They get treated with kid gloves. It's the absence of opportunity. It's stealth discrimination.

One of the executives we interviewed described her encounter with stealth discrimination. "There was a conference I wanted to go to. I asked my boss's assistant to book my ticket. She said, 'I'll have to get that cleared, because the boss doesn't let women travel alone.' This was in 2010, not 1920. In his mind, he was 'taking care of' the women in his organization. In my view he was keeping us from growing."

What makes paternalistic bias difficult to address is that it is often seemingly innocent. Generations have different values, and times have changed. Workplaces now include a greater diversity of employees, whose variations in age, gender, culture, and values require all leaders to be more sensitive to the messages they send. What once might have been protective and favorable is now seen as offensive. What once might have been chivalrous and complimentary is now viewed as condescending. But stealth discrimination isn't only a generational shift. It exists in the assumptions people make about each other and the decisions they make on those assumptions that disadvantage someone else.

Most people wouldn't even recognize themselves in the descriptions, but we hear it all the time, from the women we've coached, interviewed, and met in our work with executive teams. Examples include:

- Women who somehow end up with the low-profile, low-reward, or high-risk assignments.
- Women who are kindly asked to do administrative tasks no matter how senior they are.
- Women who are protected from pressure-filled or prime positions because of a fear that they might decide to have children, go on maternity leave, and not return.
- Women who aren't given the tough feedback they need to help them grow.

What's even more difficult to address are the unstated, paternalistic assumptions made about women that predetermine their fate. They sound like this:

- "She wouldn't want a job that required a relocation."
- "Those hours wouldn't work for her family life."
- "Women don't want that kind of role."
- "She just got married and will probably be starting a family soon. She probably wants to keep her responsibilities light."
- "Putting a woman in that role right now would be a risk."
- "That job could never be done part-time."

Fortunately, many executives and CEOs not only disagree with stealth discrimination but they also recognize it and refuse to tolerate it, simply by creating the expectation of a balanced leadership team and establishing a culture in which everyone can thrive. It would be fairer to assume that the leaders in your organization have this perspective that they don't. The last thing we want to do is to blame people who are an active part of the solution. In contrast, stealth discrimination is an insidious form of bias. To uncover it requires a heightened awareness—an awareness all leaders should build. Otherwise, they become complicit and complacent, and the bias continues.

Bad Behavior

The really bad behavior—the sexual assaults, the blatant chauvinism, the offensive attitudes, and the nasty jokes—for these, the blame needs to be ascribed where it belongs: squarely on the shoulders of the offender.

Some of these cases are more ignorant than offensive, like belittling word choice or inappropriate humor. A lot of times people don't realize their mistakes, which fall more into the category of poor taste than bad behavior. They are greatly reduced in number when the reactions they get from others in the room show them they've crossed a line—which is why men and women need to be able to react quickly to such breaches of social acceptability and snuff it out.

The more severe incidents break formal and informal policy, like withholding information or creating unfair advantages. The worst of them cross into criminality, including any kind of harassment or assault. Addressing these instances is often a group effort. The perpetrators wouldn't be acting in these ways if they were held accountable, and that may require reporting the behavior to their superiors, involving a human resource partner, or even a legal intervention.

This kind of accountability doesn't happen nearly enough. In professional circles, instances of bias tend to be taboo. But scratch the surface and ask an executive woman whether she has ever heard of, witnessed, or experienced bad behavior, and you'll find out just how prevalent it is.

Yet, for this book, we reviewed dozens of books on women in leadership, and do you know how many of them mention bad behavior? Not one. The silence is deafening. Our experts here are the women we've interviewed or coached who have seen the situations firsthand.

- They've told us about a female CEO who bragged from the stage at a worldwide management meeting about her tech company's "no tolerance" policy against discrimination, when many people knew the company had settled a multimillion dollar sexual harassment case.

Although the woman who was attacked had left the company, the perpetrator was still on the payroll.

- They've shown us obscene pictures and objects left on the desks of senior-ranking executive women.
- They've described sexist comments and innuendos that left nothing to the imagination.

It would be nice if we could brush stories like these off as extreme examples of circumstances that don't happen much these days, and we might except that our data show us otherwise. To say they are threatening to women would be an understatement. But while nothing we can say will make these situations right, at least we can provide some perspective to deal with them and provide a point of entry for discussion and change.

The Awareness Advantage

Companies and their leaders *can* learn to identify and address bias in their cultures. Whether we're talking about institutionalized bias, paternalistic discrimination, or plain old bad behavior, a little education goes a long way—and so does a culture of intolerance. Companies that address this well develop a reputation internally and/or externally for being a great place for women to work. Meanwhile, for women, the awareness advantage is the ability to be able to prevent bias if we can or handle it when we can't.

First, though, they'll have to give people the education, information, and insight to address the topic.

1. One main reason people don't address bias is because they're not conscious of it. That's why awareness is such an advantage.
2. The other reason people don't address bias is they don't know how, find it hard, don't feel it's welcome, have gotten clear feedback that it's *not* welcome, or believe it can even be dangerous.

This is a topic to approach with sensitivity and caution.

One of the solutions we've found is to shine a light on the "bright spots"—instances of leaders stepping up to be part of the solution. Some positive examples from our interviews of how leaders have handled situations to turn them into opportunities to promote a more fair, balanced, and inclusive world are as follows.

- **Firing a client.** The male founder of a $1 billion hedge fund and his female marketing executive were having drinks at a conference when a broker from a prominent investment bank spotted them and joined them. It was clear he'd had a drink or two. He sat a little too close to the woman and started questioning why she was still single. The founder of the hedge fund immediately jumped into the conversation and started listing the credentials of his colleague. He then quickly asked for the check and suggested they leave. At the founder's request, the firm ended its relationship with the broker. By making this decision, the founder signaled to others in the firm that he wouldn't do business with people and firms who mistreat employees no matter what the cost to the fund. Best execution—a term used in the trading world—was not related merely to best price but to ethics as well.

- **Including women.** A group of young male directors at a well-known Silicon Valley company invited a male senior vice president to play golf. The executive agreed on the condition they include at least one woman in the group of four. They did, and it turned into a day of building ties for everyone involved. In addition, it communicated to the younger male generation that they need to be more inclusive.

- **Arranging role models.** One CEO could see a talented woman who reported to him didn't have enough senior role models. He introduced her to two high-profile leaders who were women and set them up for lunch. By deciding to open up his contacts for his female employees, he showed how much he valued them and worked directly to help them succeed.

- **Drawing the line with between funny and offensive.** One manager had a bawdy sales team whose joking was going too far. He tamped it down with a friendly reminder. ("Hey, guys—you can't say that.") When one of them teased him ("Can't a guy have a little fun around here?"), the manager didn't smile back. ("Not if you want to work here.") The message was clear.

- **Pointing out oversights.** Two women in high-ranking leadership positions were treated like second-class citizens by the men with whom they were traveling—left out of reservations, missed on an important meeting invite, and so on. One of the women pulled one of the men aside and said, "I don't know if you've caught this, but so far on this trip you have failed to include the whole team three times. I'm sure it's an oversight, and I didn't want to make a big deal of it, but you're going to need to be more cognizant of that. It doesn't look good to the clients and it doesn't reflect well on any of us if we're not coordinated. I know it's important to you that this event goes well." Her colleague, feeling genuinely embarrassed, apologized and promised to be more inclusive from then on.

When it comes to fighting discrimination, women can't do this alone. Men need to champion women, too.

You may not be able to eliminate bias and bad behavior, but you can certainly help. Your ability to make good decisions and be a force for change will encourage others to do the same.

The Benefits of Awareness

When business leaders are able to recognize bias, they can address it or respond to it appropriately and, in the best case scenarios, move past it or even help to change it. Instances of discrimination of every kind become unacceptable. As a result, barriers are eliminated that in the past blocked their ability to succeed.

In the best cases, businesses align themselves to the ethics of awareness:

- A culture of safety, fairness, and respect.
- A business built on talent, results, performance, and opportunity for all.

Ultimately, companies committed to these principles root out bias and stamp it out.

Our Perspectives

Howard

Although it might not be popular, I want to take this opportunity to present some alternative perspectives.

It's Not Just the Men

There's no doubt discrimination is unacceptable. There's no justification for any type of bias. In the spirit of the rest of this book, however, let's remember there is always another angle. What happens if we turn these situations around?

If a woman was a CEO and promoted only men, would it be perceived the same as if the CEO were a man with an all-male team?

If a married woman was having an affair at the office, would it be equally troubling?

If I told you some of the women in the drunken events were actually throwing the parties, would that change your perspective?

I'm not saying it makes it right to reverse the situations. It's more accurate to say they're both wrong. But we do need to be careful about who we blame when anyone can engage in bad behavior. It's the *action* that needs to be put under the microscope—not the gender.

Remember How Far We've Come, and How Fast

I believe strongly in the advancement of women. I've championed many women in my career, sometimes at significant risk to myself. I'm on the side of talented women. I want them to succeed.

When I hear the cries for balance in the boardroom, though, I have to remember how far we've come. Is it far enough? No. Are organizational cultures still heavily led by men, as well as the corporate offices and boardrooms? Yes, they are.

You have to remember that this culture and these male perspectives have been in place for centuries. Women only started joining companies in larger numbers 40 or 50 years ago. It may not be happening fast enough, and it may not be good enough for one woman to be on the board, or two, or a third of the board. But it's a lot better than zero, and it wasn't that long ago there were no women at all.

The message isn't, "Be patient, change takes time." The message is, "Change is happening, and it's happening now." Let's keep going and speed up the pace.

One More Perspective

As a man, I want to go out on a limb and put forth one more viewpoint.

As we're trying to get men and corporate cultures to embrace the diversity that women and all people bring, it can actually be tough for the men to change, because it's no longer safe for them to speak up. Men have learned over the years that they can't speak their mind freely about women for fear they're going to get themselves in trouble.

Men may feel they can't be tough on a woman. They may feel they can't be honest with her about what needs to change. They know they might get it wrong. They've learned they can get sued. They're aware they could lose their jobs.

Yes, these outdated perceptions need to change, but as we're making changes, let's make sure it's safe for men to learn.

Joelle

Different forms of discriminatory situations require different approaches.

Addressing Institutionalized Bias

When it comes to institutionalized bias, awareness can work wonders. It has been well established that the solution to a problem requires the awareness of the problem and the acceptance that it exists. Many well-intentioned people carry out the systems and processes that are in place, completely unaware of how skewed they are in one direction.

You can help facilitate awareness by pointing out any inequities you see.

Most leaders don't want this kind of bias to exist. They want their companies to be fair. They want their leadership to be balanced. They want companies to provide opportunity and mobility. They want to be part of a 21st-century world in a country inspired by the notion that we are all created equal. The notion that the very companies they lead are part of the problem is startling to them.

But you can't solve a problem if you pretend it doesn't exist. You don't have to take the *blame*. This isn't your *fault*. You didn't create the system and you didn't mean for it to work against others. I'm not just talking to men here—women, too, are part of the system. Maybe you can't go back and undo the damage of the past, but you can create fairer cultures for the future.

Addressing Stealth Discrimination

Stealth discrimination is also often unconscious and equally often innocent. That's not an excuse, but it is a reason to handle it gently.

How do you address the situation if you sense you're being inhibited by an unenlightened boss? It's delicate. You don't want to come across as attacking or accusatory. The best advice we heard from women who handle this kind of situation well was not necessarily to address it in the moment, but to wait until the time is right and plan the conversation when you can go in with the right frame of mind. One executive approaches it this way:

> I tell them, "This is from the heart. Do you remember what happened? I'd like to talk about that, and let me tell you why." Especially when the intent is good, when you describe what it is about a comment or situation that is objectionable, you'll be helping someone

see another perspective. They may find it surprising or embarrassing, but they'll also probably change their ways.

You might not be able to address every instance of stealth discrimination. (As one executive put it, "The hard core chauvinists, you can't say that to them.") But having the right words can help you raise the subject with people who are willing to listen.

Addressing Bad Behavior

The negative encounters experienced by the women who participated in our research are disconcerting. One would think we had moved past vulgarity and sexism in professional settings. When and if you come across one of these incidents, it can be helpful to have a plan for how you're going to deal with it, so you can move on.

- You can report the behavior.
- You can address it directly.
- You can ignore it.
- Or you can leave.

Sometimes when women describe their encounters with bias, they are cloaked in helplessness. "What can I do?" the women shrug. They're not happy about it, but they feel powerless to change it. "There's a piece of me that feels this battle can't be fought without making it bigger," said one executive. Another agreed and added, "Right now I'm just trying to survive."

More and more, women are taking that advice. Far from taking offense at what used to be a threat ("If you don't like it, you can leave."), they are proudly declaring that they *don't* like it, so they do.

If you can't live with a situation you see at work, but you also don't feel you can (or want to) say something, you always have the option to leave. As a woman in one company said to a woman in another who was offended by the good old boys' culture surrounding them. "An organization has got to want to change. If the reason they brought you into the company was because they wanted diverse opinions, you are in an incredible place at an incredible time and can be effective. If it's not on their radar screen, life is too short. There's so much more you could do in an organization that's looking for someone like you."

How you respond to these situations is strictly your choice. There's nothing you "should" be doing, although certainly other people will have their opinions. In order, it seems logical to protect yourself and protect your career, but don't protect the perpetrator. Otherwise, they'll be there to inflict the behavior on someone else.

Admittedly, these are my personal reactions to various forms of bias or the lessons I've learned about what works in corporate settings. You may disagree. You may be someone who takes a more vehement approach. We need people like you. You may be someone who handles things more quietly—say, by simply choosing to leave one company and joining another that treats you fairly. That's okay, too. Others will disagree with me and say women should be more forceful or should be more vocal, and they may be right. You have options for how to work around the barriers, break through them, or tear them down.

You may never have an encounter like these of your own. We certainly hope not. Just the same, women need to be aware of the subtle, even unconscious forms of discrimination that surround us so we can make conscious choices about how to respond.

Q&A with Howard and Joelle

When I think about the different kinds of bias that might exist, it makes me wonder how I'd respond. What do you recommend?

Howard: It's something we all need to think about. How you respond will depend on the circumstances and the players, for certain. It will also depend somewhat on the support you have, and your ability to withstand some heat.

Here are some questions that can help you find your own answers.

- What are your guiding principles when it comes to bias?
- What are your values?
- If you assume and act as if no bias exists in your company, how would you behave? What are the positives and negatives of that approach?
- If you believe there are instances of bias and speak up, what are the positives and negatives of that approach?
- What are you willing to do, and what are you not willing to do?
- What are you afraid of? Is your fear justified?
- What can you do that makes a difference and doesn't put you, your reputation or your career at risk?
- If you don't act directly in a situation involving discrimination, is there something more you could do?

It would be nice if there were easy answers, but these aren't easy issues. Your willingness to ask the questions—and the willingness of every other man and woman—is what makes things change.

It's discouraging to think of discrimination at work. Some of this I hadn't even realized. Are things getting better?

Joelle: I have seen many instances of things getting better. While it's important to shine a light into the dark corners to help spark change, it's also important to highlight the areas where things are working.

- Executive men have started to realize they care just as much as women about being the kind of people who live in an equal world. They don't want to perpetuate bad behavior, either, and some of them have taken great pride in becoming supporters of change.
- Companies are competing now to be Best Places for Women to Work.
- Leadership development programs for women and networking groups for inclusion and diversity are springing up to prepare more people to be successful.
- Corporate policies are being examined and changed to eliminate bias.
- Journalists and the media have started exposing companies and practices that appear biased as a way of opening them up to critique and accountability.

Women are becoming savvier and stronger, too. One woman we interviewed recently attending a large dinner event hosted by a business publication. There must have been 500 women in the room. The president of the organization, speaking from the podium, proudly announced that within five years he wanted to see 20 percent of the content aligned to the priorities of women. She was stunned. Women around her were stunned. Why wait five years? And why only 20 percent? Instead of sitting still, she hollered out, "TRIPLE IT!"

Tamara: The End of the Story

After she understood just how far her company and the executive team had to go before there would be progress in achieving a balanced leadership team, Tamara decided she'd better get educated. She joined an executive roundtable on the topic of women in leadership. She learned more about hidden bias and how to address it. She started brainstorming and planning for how to make a difference. Who were the women interested in taking an active role for change? Who were the men on board who could be influencers and decision makers? What approaches to elevating women as leaders would fit best for her organization?

Tamara herself became an executive sponsor of an employee networking group for women—then she realized that wasn't enough. She circled around to each of the senior men on the leadership team and got them to sponsor the women. Each of the men has taken on two women to mentor and sponsor, and in a playful manner have even started boasting cheerfully of their wins when one of the women they have supported takes a step up in her career. Now instead of being a black mark on their record, Tamara's company is becoming recognized for their efforts to promote women.

The world *is* changing. Many companies do have women on their boards, as CEOs, on their executive committees, and throughout their org charts. They have programs advancing women. They are embracing diversity, changing their culture, and developing no-tolerance policies for discrimination of any kind.

The stories of discrimination may be disheartening, but they're not the only stories out there. As a woman who is talented, committed, and achieving in your work, you are proof of that fact.

Key Points

1. Instances of discrimination run along a continuum, from the subtle to the extreme.
2. Women are affected by bias at every level of an organization.
3. Companies and their leaders can learn to identify and address bias in their leaders, employees, systems, policies, processes, practices, and culture. Companies that address this well develop a reputation internally and/or externally for being a great place for women to work.
4. One main reason people don't address bias is because they're not conscious of it. The other reason people don't address bias is that they don't know how.
5. When it comes to fighting discrimination, women can't do this alone. Men need to champion women, too.

Questions for Reflection

1. When it comes to addressing bias, where do you stand? Would you be more likely to address situations as they arise, to ignore them, to accept them, or to walk away?
2. If you encounter bias in action, what will you do? Who will you confide in? What will you say?
3. If you witness or hear of discrimination involving someone else, what might you do to help address it or change the culture that ignores or permits such behavior?

4. What norms or patterns do you see in your organization that you think need to change? Where are the bright spots?
5. How can you take actions that are consistent with your values and give you a way to live within—and perhaps improve—the business world in which you live? What perspective brings you empowerment and peace of mind?

Conclusion:
The Next Level—
Balanced Leadership for
Better Business

"Successful organizations of the future will be led by fully engaged, balanced teams of men and women working together synergistically to produce extraordinary results."
—Rebecca Shambaugh, author of *Make Way for Her: Why Companies Need an Integrated Leadership Model to Achieve Extraordinary Results*

Revisiting Elizabeth: The End of the Story

Elizabeth was a senior vice president at a global software company who was frustrated that she simply couldn't seem to advance her career no matter how hard she tried. She eventually left her company to seek better luck, someplace else.

And she did. As she started taking leadership of her career, she became the executive vice president for one company—a competitor, and ultimately took her seat as a CEO. She got a huge salary increase, moved to Europe, and continued to build a successful, fulfilling career. Good news for Elizabeth.

Not good news for her company, or frankly, for women in leadership. It's not a win–win if every time a woman wants to advance her career, she has to find a new organization.

Contrast that with the experience of Michelle.

In her career, Michelle appeared to be following in Elizabeth's footsteps. Like Elizabeth, she reached a point in her career where the promotions

seemed to stop. Instead of moving to another company, though, she deci-
ded to take a different path.

In her executive coaching sessions, Michelle embraced The Nine
Advantages one by one.

1. *She found a new way to network—on her schedule and with the people she valued most.*
2. *She defined what success meant to her, at work and in all areas of her life.*
3. *She found mentors and enlisted sponsors.*
4. *She became conscious of her presence and learned to make a stronger impression.*
5. *She focused on her performance and prioritized her results.*
6. *She strengthened her impact and learned to communicate her results so she would be recognized.*
7. *She focused on preparing for and anticipating (instead of fixating on) the next promotion.*
8. *Along the way, she made a habit of collecting feedback to be sure she was on track.*
9. *Finally, she made the decision to work in a company that valued women—where she could see a career path and a commitment to the kind of diversity that makes good companies great.*

In the end, she felt happy and relaxed, confident in herself and in her work. She eventually worked her way up. She is now a well-regarded executive woman in a senior-level role and a leader in her company, who is actively making it a better place for women to work.

Throughout this book, we have done our best to think through the aspects of women's working lives and identify some of the barriers you are likely to encounter. Knowing the dilemmas, you can resolve them. You become empowered by committing to lead yourself, gaining mastery over who you are, what you do, how you're perceived, and how you respond to circumstances, so you can shape them in a positive way. Revisiting the question of why it's important to have women in leadership, the answer is clear: they bring a valuable perspective, and businesses need them there to compete in a global market.

In this chapter, we share our closing thoughts—closing thoughts for you as well as for business leaders and organizations.

Closing Thoughts for You

In this book, we have focused almost exclusively on how you, personally, can address the dilemmas facing you as a woman in leadership. We want you to be powerful, strong, thoughtful, and informed. You have great opportunity to shape your own experience. The new advantage for women in leadership is knowing you can empower yourself to achieve in your career and take leadership in your own life.

Nevertheless, we need to acknowledge there are circumstances women cannot change themselves. We are surrounded by a greater organizational and societal context, with challenges outside our control.

Three Layers in the Landscape

DeAnne Aguirre is a global leader at the Katzenbach Center, Strategy&, as well as a thought leader and an expert in leadership. She reminded us that there are three levels at which all of the dilemmas exist: the personal level, the organizational level, and the societal level.

Personal. At the personal level, each of us individually can make our decisions for ourselves. This is where we are most empowered. This is where we lead our own lives. We can become conscious of the ways in which we hold ourselves back, identify the instances in which we feel blocked by external barriers, and address them with clarity and confidence.

Organizational. On the organizational level, there are structures and cultures that can either perpetuate or improve on our societal norms. At times we may be able to influence organizational challenges, such as when we point out that certain policies favor some populations over others, or when we ask questions and make suggestions to shape decisions made about everything from job requirements to flex time to transparency in feedback. Other times, we may only be able to observe the realities of organizational life and how they either work for us or against us.

Societal. Although recently dialogue is increasing and gaining traction, on the societal level, we are dealing with decades, in some cases centuries, of old patterns of thought and behavior. In current decades, the traditional roles of men and women have changed. There are still places in the world where women can't hold property, go out in public without a man's permission or chaperoning, or feel safe walking down the street.

Fortunately, in developed countries such practices have disappeared, but attitudes about men (as breadwinners, decision makers, and protectors) and women (as homemakers and supporters) still exist overtly and covertly in many corners of society. We can't always change others' ways of thinking. We *can* play our part in inspiring change.

As you think about addressing the challenges you face in your future, consider the source. Is it a personal challenge, an organizational challenge, or a societal challenge? Doing so can give you some perspective, allowing you to avoid finger-pointing or feeling like a victim, and instead to focus your efforts where you can make the biggest impact.

Leaders All Around You

When we coach women, particularly in masterminds or leadership development programs that bring women together as a group, one of the most common comments we hear from our participants is, "Now I know I'm not alone."

You're not alone. Even if you're the only woman at the table in your organization, you're not alone. You're surrounded by other women in other organizations that are also working toward success and change, just like you.

You're also surrounded by executive women in other parts of your organization, executive men sitting at the table with you, and men and women at every level who want to enjoy meaning, joy, balance, and a sense of success in their careers—and who want the same for you.

Closing Thoughts for Business Leaders and Organizations

The new advantage for companies that value women in leadership and commit to balancing their leadership teams with both women *and* men is that they will be well positioned to lead in the future.

We're Headed for Change. In Some Places, We're Already There

In our experience, both men and women want to see a more balanced corporate culture. The culture is quickly changing. The truth is that the business culture isn't even all "male" anymore. It's becoming more gender balanced, generationally rich, and culturally diverse every day.

Today's young men and women value diversity. They value their quality of life. They also share their responsibilities. Women are joining executive teams and board meetings, and men are dropping kids off to school on their way to work. Men are asking themselves the same questions as women about how to balance their lives along with their careers.

> Not all men want the same thing, of course . . . But in the professional ranks, a new organization man has indeed emerged, one who wants to be an involved father with no loss of income, prestige, and corporate support—and no diminished sense of manhood. Like working women, we want it all.[1]

Men and women come at it from different histories, but in large part they want the same thing: a happy, full, accomplished, and meaningful life.

- Men have traditionally spent their time at work, sacrificing time at home, and the chance to raise their children.
- Women have traditionally managed the home front and struggled to gain credibility at work.

Now they are closer to merging in the middle. Perhaps the long-term result will be that books like these become obsolete as both men and women learn to better integrate their personal and professional lives. We certainly hope so.

Change Requires Commitment, Measured by Results

One of the first women we interviewed for this book, a vice president of leadership development at a large multinational insurance company, made an observation we found telling. She reported that, in her organization, the conversation about women in leadership had changed—in part, due to their efforts to support women and help them succeed in their careers.

"It's interesting," she reported. "The tone is different. Women seem more positive, more empowered. We hear less complaining. They seem to realize now that they own their careers and can do things to help themselves advance. But have the numbers changed? Are there actually more women in leadership? No."

Her comments point to the next phase needed for the advancement of women in leadership: a commitment to action, measured by results. As one astute client of ours observed, "We would never accept this kind of failure if we were talking about profits instead of people. For some reason the lack of progress in this area continues to be acceptable."

Perhaps there was a time corporate leaders could do what they wanted with little accountability to the outside world. Indeed, some executives still try to operate in this manner. Shareholders, employees, customers, and the global community are demanding more. They have expectations of transparency and the technology to attain it. The old insular management model no longer works. In addition to the fact that today's society values diversity, the research indicates that balanced leadership leads to better business, and corporate leaders whose job it is to improve profitability need to embrace the changes that make their companies perform as best they can.

With a savvy workforce in a digital age, there's no hiding anymore. With a glimpse at the web site, prospective employees, clients, and competitors can see for themselves whether a company values its women. The board members' photos are there on the web site for all to see. Business publications honor companies that are best places for women to work and, by omission, discredit the rest. In response, women *and* customers are voting with their feet. They're walking out and finding companies where they feel valued.

The Necessity of Women

Of all the efforts designed to bring better balance to leadership, there's one that makes the biggest difference. We simply have to have more women at the top. Women need to be included in the efforts to open up more senior leadership positions to women, and organizations need to change to incorporate their views. Women are the ones who understand the challenges from the inside out. They are the ones who can identify the barriers and make suggestions to help companies move them away. It's the outcome we've been talking about throughout this book, but it's also the solution.

We got a glimpse of how many of the challenges we've been discussing melt away when we talked to leaders in companies who *have* balanced leadership teams. One executive we interviewed with had been at her company for 30 years, starting as a director and ending her career as the CEO—one of the few in the Fortune 500. Early in her career, she experienced the dilemmas, felt sidelined, and was disadvantaged. Over the years, her company worked hard to change, adding employee networking groups, mentoring programs, and women's initiatives. Finally, in recent years, the board and the executive committee had created what we've been advocating throughout this book: balanced leadership teams of men and women. The result was remarkable. Suddenly, the tension and the striving that had characterized conversations about women in leadership gave way to an easier, more settled, more mature culture reflective of 21st-century life. As the CEO said,

> We didn't have to talk about change anymore. Things changed. They changed, because *we* changed.

Her sentiments were echoed in other companies where the CEO was a woman, or the executive committee was balanced, or the board of directors had equal numbers of men and women. Their experience that the changes happen naturally once the leadership teams arrive at an initial balance lends further urgency to the objective of moving women into leadership roles, because having them there will create a critical mass and accelerate the change.

If you want to have women in leadership, you have to have women in leadership.

In many ways, that's what we're looking for. After all the talk about what women want, the truth is they want to move past that question altogether. Ultimately, "women's leadership development programs" and "best places for women to work" will become obsolete. Putting women into senior leadership roles won't be a "risk," and we'll no longer need "a business case for women in leadership." (Can you imagine having to make a business case for men?) Women will stop being singled out.

> Asking "what women want" is like asking what zebras want, or what politicians want. Their individual wants are as different from those of other women just as they're the same as those of many men. . . . There may be more similarities than differences between men and women when it comes to defining success.[2]

Stormy Simon, the president of Overstock.com, made a comment common to many of the women we've interviewed: "I hope the next generation won't even know this challenge existed." As more women are advanced into leadership positions, their numbers reach a tipping point and that's when change will finally take place.

The sooner we can get there, the easier this will be.

The Importance of Men

A critical discovery to come out of our research is the significance of men in the advancement of women. In part, it's because that's still where much of the power lies. In part, it's because men understand the rules of corporate life—the unstated rules about how to succeed in a culture built largely by men. In part, it's because it's too complex a challenge for a small subset of leaders to accomplish alone. Both men and women must be involved.

Otherwise, the entire effort lands on the shoulders of women and those who have carried those efforts will tell you it can be a heavy burden. As one of our clients said, "It gets old being the only woman and the only advocate of women."

It's not just because women are tired of fighting. It's also because it's damaging for women to press the issue all of the time. They can become known as instigators, no matter how right they are.

As one of our research participants said, "If you look at the number of women in senior management positions and board level positions, there's no way you can say it's not an issue. It's not possible to ignore that. But it is a dangerous topic to take up as a woman. It can marginalize you in an instant. There appears to be no upside for a woman to actually articulate the problem. You'll be stigmatized."

It may be risky for an individual woman to speak up, but it's a bigger risk for corporate leaders *not* to, because the betterment of the business is at stake. We have many examples of executive leaders actively working to get a better balance of women in leadership.

- At Adobe, executive vice president of Worldwide Field Operations, Matt Thompson, studied data that showed how many women held leadership positions at his company, compared to men. He realized they could do better and set out to change that. He engaged the Leadership Research Institute (LRI) to work with his organization to bring women together, build them as leaders, and encourage them to move up in the company. As a result, women are opting into leadership roles and contributing to the success of the company while advancing their own careers.
- At MetLife, Executive Vice President Tony Nugent has instituted the annual Women's Sales Summit to help sales women advance their careers and move into management. Similarly, Executive Vice President Mike Vietri sponsored LRI's Leadership Circles Program to create a network of high-performing women around the country. In part, as a result of these efforts, MetLife was named a *Best Company for Women to Work*.[3]
- At MGM Resorts, senior executives have sponsored Employee Networking Groups, led by the then vice president of Diversity and Inclusion,

Ondra Berry. As part of a broader series aimed at expanding diversity of all kinds, two of these groups are targeted specifically for women: one for women in general and the other specifically for working mothers. By sponsoring the groups, leaders on the executive committee lend credibility and visibility to the effort.

Not surprisingly, women in our research are excited about the companies that are "loud and proud" about their efforts to support women and see them as inviting places for talented women to build their careers. Matt Thompson, executive vice president of WorldWide Field Operations at Adobe, confirms that the investment is well spent:

> We want to attract the best talent in the market. When we provide an environment that supports women's continued growth and development, our female employees are even more engaged and will continue to recruit exceptional talent into the company. When you love your job, you'll be good at it . . . so it helps drive [our] business. It's a double win.

Our hope is that efforts like these will culminate into a balanced corporate culture—one in which women and their companies benefit equally from having women in leadership.

Until then, a focus on women should remain an integral part of leadership development and talent management. The ability for women to succeed as corporate leaders depends largely on the investment, sponsorship, and active engagement of men in leadership positions committed to making a difference.

Our Top Three Recommendations for Advancing Women in Leadership

We've talked in this book about what you can do to excel and advance your own career. Now you have the opportunity to become a leader in helping others do the same. On an organizational level, we have three top recommendations for advancing women in leadership.

Share The New Advantage

We wrote this book to find a vehicle for communicating with more leaders and coaching them in overcoming the challenges they face in their careers. If it's helped you, it will help others, so pass it along. More importantly, however, you can use this book to connect with other leaders like you and strengthen your efforts toward change—change for you, change for each other, and change for your organization. You will have more ideas, courage, and a stronger voice with other leaders than you will have alone.

- **Read and discuss this book with others.** The examples, points, and questions posed in this book are intended to spark discussion, so you can personalize your learning and make decisions about your actions. This book will be more effective when leaders read it together and discuss what they discover in light of their own experience.
- **Host a discussion.** Gather a group of leaders to discuss some of the insights you've gained.
- **Share the strategies.** Pull out questions or exercises from the book and use them to develop other leaders or to succeed in your initiatives.

Let this book be a resource for you—an active, interactive set of tools for building a successful career.

Encourage Executive Coaching

Because the dilemmas are still not always safe topics for conversation, the confidentiality of executive coaching and its deeply personal, entirely individualized nature make it an ideal environment for working through the challenges that inevitably accompany leadership development and taking advantage of the opportunities ahead.

Of course, as executive coaches we're biased here. More than enough evidence suggests, executive coaching is an invaluable tool to increasing the presence of women at the corporate executive level. One McKinsey report found that the opportunity to work with an external coach was identified as "by far the most valuable component" of the leadership programs they studied.[4] In our own research at the LRI, we have found that executive coaching for executive women has resulted directly in promotions. In one study, over 85 percent of the female senior-level leaders we have coached were promoted within the first 6 months of beginning their coaching, and almost all of them advanced within the year.

Offer Leadership Development Programs for Women in Leadership

Programs that teach the skills and strategies of leadership provide the opportunity for learning and discussion about the challenges facing women and men in the workplace. The challenges are critical for *all* aspiring leaders to understand—not just for women.

Leadership development programs can be part of a comprehensive strategy that companies adopt to integrate the development of talented leaders with the goals of their companies to promote their advancement.

Elements of such programs might include:

- Live events
- Virtual sessions
- Small group discussions
- Masterminds
- Peer coaching.

Through this variety of approaches, members participate from multiple, even global locations. The effect is the formation of cohorts of confident leaders who are successfully navigating the pace, culture, and expectations of life as a leader while preserving a sense of personal and professional well-being.

To give a sense of the results, in one of our programs for 30 women,

- Individual performance measures related to participants goals' included increases in productivity, sales, or other measures of performance from 45 percent to 400 percent.
- Over 93 percent reported that a strategic, reflective approach had come to characterize their leadership.
- The number of participants consistently maintaining peak performance and balancing a healthy quality of life both on and off the job doubled by the end of the program.
- Up to six members were promoted during the span of the program.

As you consider ways to share the learnings from *The New Advantage*, whether you're considering informal gathering, formal executive coaching, or large-scale leadership development program, just let us know how we can help. That's why we're here.

You

You are a highly accomplished woman, considered to be of the top performing women in your company. You are a leader. You're excited about your career so far, and you're inspired to be a part of the leadership team—one of the increasingly vibrant and balanced leadership teams your company has ever had, in part, thanks to the advancement of women like you. You commit yourself to resolving whatever dilemmas may present themselves, so you can achieve your vision for yourself as a leader. You and your company have created a win–win—a way for you to take full advantage of the benefits of women in leadership.

As you now continue to advance your career, it is our hope that you have a new set of perspectives, knowledge, and strategies for supporting women in leadership—starting with yourself.

Key Points

1. The new advantage for women in leadership is knowing you can empower yourself to achieve in your career and take leadership in your own life.
2. The new advantage for companies that value women in leadership and commit to balancing their leadership teams with both women *and* men is that they will be well positioned to lead in the future.
3. There are circumstances women cannot change themselves. We can't always change others' ways of thinking. We *can* play our part in inspiring change.
4. The culture is quickly changing. It's becoming more gender balanced, generationally rich, and culturally diverse every day.
5. The next phase needed for the advancement of women in leadership is a commitment to action, measured by results.

Questions for Reflection

1. What do you see as your next step?
2. What step do you think is next for your organization?
3. How can you make that happen?

Notes

Introduction

1. Sheryl Sandberg, *Lean In: Women, Work and the Will to Lead* (New York: Knopf, 2013).

2. Catalyst, "Women CEOs of the S&P 500," Catalyst.org, April 3, 2015, http://www.catalyst.org/knowledge/women-ceos-sp-500 (accessed August 28, 2015).

3. Joanna Barsh and Lareina Yee, "Changing Companies' Minds about Women," *McKinsey Quarterly*, 2011, http://www.mckinsey.com/insights/organization/changing_companies_minds_about_women.

4. Catalyst, "Women CEOs of the S&P 500."

5. Sue Shellenbarger, "The XX Factor: What's Holding Women Back?" *The Wall Street Journal*, May 7, 2012, http://www.wsj.com/articles/SB10001424052702304746604577381953238775784.

6. Catalyst, "The Bottom Line: Connecting Corporate Performance and Gender Diversity," Catalyst.org, January 15, 2004, http://www.catalyst.org/knowledge/bottom-line-connecting-corporate-performance-and-gender-diversity.

7. Roy D. Adler, "Women in the Executive Suite Correlate to High Profits," Pepperdine University, 2001, http://www.csripraktiken.se/files/adler_web.pdf.

8. Rebecca Shambaugh, *Make Room for Her: Why Companies Need an Integrated Model of Leadership to Achieve Extraordinary Results* (New York: McGraw Hill, 2012).

9. Ibid.

10. Adler, "Women in the Executive Suite."

11. Catalyst, "The Bottom Line."

12. McKinsey & Company, "Women Matter: Gender Diversity, a Corporate Performance Driver," October 2007, http://www.mckinsey.com/~/media/McKinsey/dotcom/client_service/Organization/PDFs/Women_matter_oct2007_english.ashx.

13. Georges Desvaux, Sandrine Devillard-Hoellinger, and Mary C. Meaney, "A Business Case for Women," *The McKinsey Quarterly*, October 2008.

14. Bob Sherwin, "Why Women Are More Effective Leaders than Men," Business Insider, January 24, 2014, http://www.businessinsider.com/study-women-are-better-leaders-2014-1.

15. Marti Barletta, *Marketing to Women: How to Understand, Reach, and Increase Your Share of the World's Largest Market Segment* (Chicago: Dearborn Trade Publishing, 2002).

16. Claire Shipman and Katty Kay, *Womenomics* (New York: Harper Business, 2009).

17. Wendy Kaufman, "Women Still Largely Absent from Corporate Boards," National Public Radio, December 10, 2013, http://www.npr.org/2013/12/10/249862083/women-still-largely-absent-from-corporate-boards.

18. Joanna Barsh and Lareina Yee, "Unlocking the Potential of Women in the U.S. Economy," McKinsey & Company, April 2011, http://www.mckinsey.com/client_service/organization/latest_thinking/unlocking_the_full_potential.

19. "Fulfilling the Promise; How More Women on Corporate Boards Would Make America and American Companies More Competitive," Washington, DC, The Committee for Economic Development, https://www.ced.org/reports/single/fulfilling-the-promise.

20. Catalyst, "The Bottom Line."

21. Claire Braund, "Why Women Are Good for Business," Women on Boards, December 2011, http://www.womenonboards.org.au/pubs/articles/1112-why-women-are-good-for-business.htm.

22. Joelle K. Jay, *The Inner Edge: The 10 Practices of Personal Leadership* (Santa Barbara, CA: Praeger, 2009).

Chapter 1

1. Ivan Misner, Hazel M. Walker, and Frank J. De Raffelle Jr., *Business Networking and Sex (Not What You Think)* (Irvine, CA: Entrepreneur Press, 2012).

2. Ibid.

Chapter 2

1. Joanna Barsh, Susie Cranston, and Rebecca A. Craske, "Centered Leadership: How Talented Women Thrive," *The McKinsey Quarterly*, September 2008, http://www.mckinsey.com/insights/leading_in_the_21st_century/centered_leadership_how_talented_women_thrive.

2. Bryce Covert, "Women Around the World Do More Work Each Week and Have Less Time for Themselves," *ThinkProgress.org*, November 5, 2013, http://thinkprogress.org/economy/2013/11/05/2891951/women-work-time-oecd/.

3. Daniel Goleman, Richard Boyatzis, and Annie McKee, *Primal Leadership: Unlocking the Power of Emotional Intelligence* (Boston, MA: Harvard Business Review Press, 2013).

4. Claire Shipman and Katty Kay, *Womenomics* (New York: Harper Business, 2009).

5. Joelle K. Jay, *The Inner Edge: The 10 Practices of Personal Leadership* (Santa Barbara, CA: Praeger, 2009).

6. Sharon Meers and Joanna Strober, *Getting to 50/50: How Working Couples Can Have It All by Sharing It All* (New York: Bantam Books, 2009).

7. Sylvia Ann Hewlett, Kerri Peraino, Laura Sherbin, and Karen Sumberg, "The Sponsor Effect: Breaking Through the Last Glass Ceiling," *Harvard Business Review*, January 12, 2011, https://hbr.org/product/the-sponsor-effect-breaking -through-the-last-glass-ceiling/an/10428-PDF-ENG.

8. Ibid.

Chapter 3

1. C. Shipman and K. Kay, *The Confidence Code: The Science and Art of Self-Assurance—What Women Should Know* (New York: Harper Business, 2014).

2. Sylvia Ann Hewlett, Kerri Peraino, Laura Sherbin, and Karen Sumberg, "The Sponsor Effect: Breaking through the Last Glass Ceiling," *Harvard Business Review*, January 12, 2011, https://hbr.org/product/the-sponsor-effect-breaking -through-the-last-glass-ceiling/an/10428-PDF-ENG.

3. Ibid.

4. Herminia Ibarra, Nancy M. Carter, and Christine Silva, "Why Men Still Get More Promotions than Women" *Harvard Business Review* (2010): 80–85.

5. K. Dodge, "Recognizing and Addressing Women's Priorities at Work," *Mobility*, 2009.

6. Hewlett et al., "The Sponsor Effect."

7. Sylvia Ann Hewlett, *Forget a Mentor, Get a Sponsor* (Boston, MA: Harvard Business Review Press, 2013).

8. Sylvia Ann Hewlett, "The Real Benefit of Finding a Sponsor," *Harvard Business Review*, January 26, 2011, https://hbr.org/2011/01/the-real-benefit-of -finding-a/.

9. Hewlett et al., "The Sponsor Effect."

Chapter 4

1. Jenna Goudreau, "Do You Have 'Executive Presence'?" *Forbes.com*, October 29, 2012, http://www.forbes.com/sites/jennagoudreau/2012/10/29/do -you-have-executive-presence/.

2. Bob Sherwin, "Why Women Vanish as They Move Up the Career Ladder," *Business Insider*, January 27, 2014, http://www.businessinsider.com/women-and -career-advancement-leadership-2014-1.

3. Suzanne Doyle-Morris, *Beyond the Boys' Club: Strategies for Achieving Career Success as a Man Working in a Male-Dominated Field* (UK: Wit and Wisdom Press, 2009).

4. Sylvia Ann Hewlett, *Forget a Mentor, Get a Sponsor* (Boston, MA: Harvard Business Review Press, 2013).

5. Ibid.

6. K. Hedges, *The Power of Presence: Unlock Your Potential to Influence and Engage Others* (New York: AMACOM, 2012).

7. Goudreau, "Do You Have 'Executive Presence'?"

Chapter 5

1. "Fulfilling the Promise; How More Women on Corporate Boards Would Make America and American Companies More Competitive," Washington, DC, The Committee for Economic Development, https://www.ced.org/reports/single /fulfilling-the-promise.

2. John Bussey, "How Women Can Get Ahead: Advice from Female CEOs," *Wall Street Journal*, May 18, 2012, http://www.wsj.com/articles/SB1000142405 27023038796045774105205112 35252.

Chapter 6

1. Rodd Wagner and James K. Harter, *12: The Elements of Great Managing* (New York: Gallup, 2006).

2. Jill Flynn, Kathryn Heath, and Mary Davis Holt, *Break Your Own Rules: How to Change Patterns of Thinking that Block Women's Path to Power* (San Francisco, CA: Jossey-Bass, 2011).

3. Georges Desvaux, Sandrine Devillard-Hoellinger, and Mary C. Meaney, "A Business Case for Women," *The McKinsey Quarterly*, October 2008.

4. J. Winter, "Not Getting Recognized for Your Work? How to Take Credit," *Huffington Post*, 2012.

5. K. Dodge, "Recognizing and Addressing Women's Priorities at Work," *Mobility*, 2009.

6. "Predictions 2014," Deloitte, 2014.

7. Mika Brzezinski, *Knowing Your Value: Women, Money, and Getting What You're Worth* (New York: Weinstein, 2010).

8. S. Cain, *Quiet: The Power of Introverts in a World that Can't Stop Talking* (New York, Broadway, 2013).

Chapter 7

1. Peggy Drexler, "What Do Career Women Want?" *Forbes.com*, September 16, 2013, http://www.forbes.com/sites/peggydrexler/2013/09/16/what-do -career-women-want/.

2. Claire Shipman and Katty Kay, *Womenomics* (New York: Harper Business, 2009).

3. Ibid.

4. Ibid.

5. Selena Rezvani, *Pushback* (San Francisco, CA: Jossey-Bass, 2012).

6. Ibid.

Chapter 8

1. Sylvia Ann Hewlett, *Forget a Mentor, Get a Sponsor* (Boston, MA: Harvard Business Review Press, 2013).

2. Ibid.

3. Sharon Meers and Joanna Strober, *Getting to 50/50: How Working Couples Can Have It All by Sharing It All* (New York: Bantam Books, 2009).

4. Marshall Goldsmith, *What Got You Here Won't Get You There* (New York: Hyperion, 2007).

5. Cathy Swody, "Survey Says: It's All about the Follow-Up," American Management Association, September 20, 2012, http://www.amanet.org/training/articles/Survey-Says-Its-All-About-the-Follow-up.aspx.

6. Joann S. Lublin, "Coaching Urged for Women," *Wall Street Journal*, April 4, 2011, http://www.wsj.com/articles/SB10001424052748704530204576237203974840800.

Chapter 9

1. Peninah Thomson and Jacey Graham, *A Woman's Place Is in the Boardroom* (New York: Palgrave Macmillan, 2005).

2. "Sexual Harassment: Myths and Realities," *The Journal of the American Psychological Association*.

3. Leslie Kwoh, "McKinsey Tries to Recruit Mothers Who Left the Fold," *Wall Street Journal*, February 19, 2013, http://www.wsj.com/articles/SB10001424127887323764804578314450063914388.

Conclusion

1. Michael S. Kimmel, "What Do Men Want?" *Harvard Business Review*, November–December 1993, https://hbr.org/1993/11/what-do-men-want.

2. Peggy Drexler, "What Do Career Women Want?" *Forbes.com*, September 16, 2013, http://www.forbes.com/sites/peggydrexler/2013/09/16/what-do-career-women-want/.

3. Joelle K. Jay, "Raising the Glass Ceiling," T&D, 2013.

4. D.J. Mitsch, "Women Use Coaching for Upward Mobility," Training Industry, Inc., February 19, 2013, https://www.trainingindustry.com/leadership/articles/women-use-coaching-for-upward-mobility.aspx.

Index

acceptance: of feedback, 64; of institutionalized bias, 153
accountability, 148, 156, 164
advancement, xix, xxii–xxiii, 12, 38, 40, 42–43, 52, 69, 76–77, 80, 84, 98, 108–119, 123, 152, 163, 165, 169–170, 178; definition, 106–107
advancement dilemma, the, 106–108
advocates, 37–38, 41, 47–50, 53, 76, 79, 83, 87, 100, 138, 166
aggression, xxii, 92
Aguirre, DeAnne, 161
ambition, 20, 36, 38, 43 68
appearance, 15, 58, 64–68, 143
appreciation, 43, 94, 110
ask: about bias, 92, 96, 102, 155; for advancement, 109, 117; the direct ask, 3, 11, 49; for examples, 80; for feedback, 62, 82, 86, 93, 101, 125, 128, 131–133, 138; for help, 39; for ideas, 30; for mentorship, sponsorship, 46–49; for raise, 43; reflective questions, 130; for the sale, 4; sharing one's needs, 33
authenticity, 60, 110
awareness: and advancement, 108, 132; advantage, 149; awareness dilemma, 142; benefits, 151; of bias, 44, 146, 148, 153; and

executive presence, 61, 64–65; political, 14; self-, 101, 131
awareness dilemma, the, 142–144

balance: achieving, 20, 23; as advancement, 111; advantage, xxv, 17–36; beliefs, 26; benefits, 23; businesses want, xviii; culture, 144, 148, 152, 162, 167; definition, 18; dilemma, 18, 26, 33; finding, xiv; home and family, 19, 24; ideas, 26; improving, xxvii–xxviii, 21, 23; leadership, xviii, xx, xxiii, 42, 141–142, 148, 153, 156, 164–166, 169; life, xxix, 19, 21–22, 27, 30–31; men and, xxvi, 30, 163; mindset, 26; perspectives, xxvi; priorities, 22; sense of, 20, 36; women want, 107; workforce, xx, xxviii, 43; work/life, 27, 32, 33
balance dilemma, the, 18–21, 26, 33
blame, xi, xxix, 63, 99, 101, 142, 148, 152–153
board of directors, xxi, 49, 165
Brzezinski, Mika, 97
Buscarino, Christine, 17
business: advancement in, xxiii; advantage, xix; and bias, 151;

business (*cont.*)
  businesses needs, xviii; case for
    women in leadership, xxi, 165;
    culture, xxii, xxix, 42, 98, 162;
    discrimination, 144; diversity,
    benefits to, xxviii, 109, 160, 164;
    impact, xix, 43; leadership, xviii,
    xx–xxi, xxvi, 41, 164, 166;
    priorities, 4; relationships, 15;
    rules of, environment, 67, 98;
    work-life balance, 23
Buzz, 95

Carone, Christa, 105
changing home environment, 24
chemistry, 44–45, 53
choice, xxix, 34, 63; in addressing
    bad behavior, 154–155; to define
    success, 107, 109; executive
    presence, 69, 74, 76; to know
    your value, 97; in response to
    feedback, 139; to stay or leave,
    113, 120–122; work and life, 20,
    26, 35
Clark, Susan, 128
comfort, 4–6, 13, 101; zone, 5, 16
commitment: to change, 163; effective
    networking, 14; employee levels
    of, 143; mentors, sponsors, 43, 46;
    self-improvement, 128, 130, 133
communication skills, 116; definition,
    60
confidence: executive presence, 59,
    68; feedback, 123, 128, 140;
    mentorship and sponsorship, 38;
    networking, 14; performance, 77;
    promotion, 111; self-, 43, 66, 134;
    work/life balance, 18, 32
control: acceptance, 101; advance-
    ment, 77, 111; executive presence,
    65; feedback, 128; over career, 46,
    108, 111–112; over life, 30, 33;
    over time, 22–23, 28; performance,
    77, 84, 118

credibility, xxvi, 61–63, 163, 167;
    advancement, 115; building, 4, 81,
    89, 91; leadership, 130
credit: sharing, 91, 95, 100; taking,
    74, 83, 90, 92–93, 99, 101, 103,
    112

data, 166; feedback, 70, 127, 130,
    136; opportunities, 85
demeanor, executive presence, 59, 86
demonstrate, 48–49; readiness, 116;
    your value, 112
Denzel, Nora, 48
development: executive development
    plan, 119, 139; leadership, 53,
    101, 162, 165, 167–169; mentor-
    ship relationship, 44, 52; personal,
    79, 126, 137; team, 80, 82
dilemma, xi, xix, xxiii–xxx, 2, 3, 82;
    addressing, 160–161; advance-
    ment, 106–108; awareness,
    142–144; balance, 18–21, 26, 33;
    definition, xxiv; discussing, 168;
    executive presence, 56–58;
    experiencing, 164; feedback,
    126–127; layers of, 161; network-
    ing, 2–3, 6; performance, 74–78;
    recognition, 90–91, 101; resolving,
    170; sponsorship, 38–39
diversity, xiii, xviii, xxviii, 6, 43, 51,
    87, 141, 145, 147, 153, 156–157,
    160, 162, 164, 167
double life, 18
Drexler, Peggy, 107

education, 65, 149
election, definition of, 84–85
empowerment, xxiv, xxviii, 158
endorsement, 8
executive coaching, ix, 10, 108, 160,
    168–169; benefit, xiv; importance,
    137; role of, 136
executive presence, xi, xxii, xxv,
    55–72, 85–86, 95, 116

executive presence dilemma, the, 56–58
expectations, xxv, 164, 169; clarifying, 98, 131; exceeding, 111; executive presence, 58, 60, 63, 70; feedback, 138; and formal programs, 51; managing, 33; others', 57; outperforming, 73–88, 91

feedback: advantage, xxv, 125–140; benefits, 131; bias, 136, 149; culture of, 128, 139–140, 161; defensiveness, 63, 70, 132, 134, 138; definition, 126, 132; executive coaching, 136–137; on executive presence, 57–58, 62–64, 71; gender and, 136–137, 147; getting, 1, 15, 52, 62–63, 70, 73, 75, 127–128, 137–138; Goldsmith, Marshall, on, 131; handling, xi, 64–65, 125–127, 132–133, 138–139; interactive reviews, 130; key points, 140; negative, 61, 65, 101, 125–126; on performance, 79–80, 85–86, 93; pitfalls, 132, 134; self-assessment, 129; 360-degree, ix, 128–129; using, 130, 133–135, 137, 139
feedback dilemma, the, 126–127
financial performance, xxi

gender, ix, xxvi, xxviii, 7, 14, 24–25, 32, 43, 46, 112, 121–122, 136, 145, 147, 152, 162, 170; bias, 121, 135; quotas, 107
gender line, 3, 5–6, 122
Gibb, Laura, 63
Glassman, Saly, 125
global competitive advantage, xxi
goals: achieving, 110, 120, 139, 141; balance, 18, 23; coaching, 119; commitment to, 114; mentorship and sponsorship, 44, 48; of networking, 6–16; performance

and, 169; practices of personal leadership, 22; professional, 20, 25, 34; setting, 6, 76, 79, 82, 109, 115–116; understanding others' 96
Goldsmith, Marshall, xi, 131

Hanna, Kim, 55
Hedges, Kristi, 59
Herda, Larissa, 60
Hewlett, Sylvia Ann, 38, 40, 50–51
human resources, xxvii, 3, 19

Ida, Doreen, 50
impact: of executive coaching, xxvii, xiv, 160; executive presence, 59–60, 64–65, 68, 71; feedback, 65, 70, 133, 135, 137–138, 139; of gender imbalance on business, xix; of networking, 3, 16; performance, 74, 81, 102; personal commitment, 48; of sponsorship, 39–40, 54
inclusion, xxvii, 156
influence, xxiii
intellect and expertise, 60
intention, xx, 84, 108, 122; bias, 145; executive presence, 59, 68; feedback, 138
interpersonal behavior patterns, 60
interpersonal skills, xxii, 60
interview-based 360-degree profile, ix, 70, 128–129, 139

Jenkins, Annalisa, 37, 40, 43
judgment, 59, 65, 120; as decision making, 64, 112; lack of blame and, xxix, 40

Kay, Katty, xx, 20, 117
Kelman, Gail, 92

leadership: advancement, 7, 56, 64, 106, 123, 163, 165, 167–170; approach to, 47; balanced

leadership (*cont.*)
    leadership, xxviii, xx, xxiii, xxvi,
    42, 148, 153, 160, 162, 164, 166;
    better lives, 21; bias against
    women in, 145, 148, 150, 153; the
    business case for women, xxi–xxii,
    165; challenges of leadership, xv,
    xviii, 41; characteristics, 145;
    complexities of female, 13;
    current, xiv; definition, xxiii;
    development program, 53, 91, 101,
    143, 156, 162, 165, 169; executive
    presence, 58–60, 63, 65; feedback
    on, 128–129; feminine approach,
    xx; good leader, 84; insecurity, 53;
    men as leaders, 43; nine advan-
    tages, xxiv–xxv; personal leader-
    ship, xxiii–xxiv, 22, 116, 159;
    recognizing, 47; senior, 112, 141,
    164, 165; shared role, 109; skills,
    114; strengthening, xx, xxii–xxiii;
    style, 98, 126, 130, 134; versus
    sponsorship, 52; women in, xv,
    xviii, xix, xx, xxiii, xxix–xxxi, 41,
    47, 54, 58, 74, 156, 161, 163, 165,
    167, 170; work/life balance and, 22
lobby, for yourself, 38, 48, 91, 97
Long, Peter, 25, 33

management: insular model, 164;
    recognition by, 93; relationships,
    89; role, 34, 106, 122, 166; senior
    positions, xix, xxxi, 34, 166;
    talent, xxviii, 116, 167; women in,
    141–142
Marcario, Rose, 128
marginalizing, 99, 166
masterminds, 162, 169
Mayer, Marissa, 76
Meers, Sharon, 25, 35
mentorship, xi, xxii, xxv; benefits of,
    43; conditions of, 44–46; defini-
    tion, 38–39, 41; getting, 38,
    46–47; maintaining, 48, 116, 131;

Mirshokrai, Camille, and, 48;
    networking, 9; over-mentored, 39;
    role of men as, 41; value of,
    39–41; versus sponsor, 39–42,
    50–51; women as, 42. *See also*
    sponsorship
meritocracy, 75, 145
Mirshokrai, Camille, 48
Morena, Christine, 3
Morris, Donna, 3
multiple points on the mountain,
    49–50
mutual benefit, 44–45

negotiation checklist, 117
networking (network): advantage,
    xxiv, 1–16; approach, 3–9;
    attitude, 4; benefits of, 2, 5;
    building, 2, 10, 12–15, 47, 49,
    116; challenges, 2; definition, 2–3;
    dilemma, 2; feedback from, 131;
    goals of, 7–8; groups, 13–14, 28,
    156, 164; importance, xi; men's,
    3–4; new kinds of, 6; perception,
    5; strategy, 2; traditional, 3, 6;
    women's, 2
networking dilemma, the, 2–3, 6
the new all, 109
Nicholson, Pam, 81
Nugent, Tony, 95, 166

objectives, 119; career, 116; setting,
    80, 116
opportunity: as advancement, 115;
    maximizing, 47–48; networking, 5,
    10, 15; saying "no" to, 31
organizational health, xxi

perception: confidence, 14; executive
    presence, 58, 71; in gender
    interactions; misperception, 79;
    networking, 5, 15–16; others', 64,
    76, 84, 132, 137; performance, 78;
    self-perception, 70

performance, 60, 70, 102; advantage, xxv, 73–88; backfire, 83; benefits, 77; coaching and, 169; definition, 74; dilemma, 74; expectations, 91; feedback, 85–86, 131; financial, xxi; impact, 81–82; Mayer, Melissa, on, 76; measures, 76, 78, 80–82, 87, 114; over-achieving, 116; perception, 78; proactive conversations, 79, 84, 86; recognizing, 79, 82–85, 87, 93–94; review, 79–80, 86, 126, 137, 139–140, 143, 145; value of, 75, 84–85, 118–119, 151; Wilderotter, Maggie, on, 76
performance dilemma, the, 74–78
perspective, xiv, xv, xvii, xxi, xxiii, xxix, 7, 8, 14, 20, 46, 66, 84, 91, 98, 108, 131, 148, 149, 151, 160, 162; on advancement, 107, 108, 123; balanced, xxvi; choosing, 107, 113, 119, 120; diversity, 6, 129; on feedback, 127; loss of, 19; men's, xxvi, 30, 101, 152; shifting, 14; women's, 6
physical characteristics, 59
power use, 60
proactive: being, 7–8; networking, 16; performance, 79; performance conversations, 79, 84, 86; sponsor, 41
promotion, xxi, 12, 18, 39, 53; advancement, 106, 109; ambivalence, 107; asking for, 91, 94–95; bias and, 144; career satisfaction, 111; executive coaching, 168; feedback, 129; focus, 112, 114; performance and, 77, 118–120; perspective of, 119, 120–121; process, 51, 113; recognition and, 97; role of men, promoting women, 41, 43, 55; success and, 110; tiara syndrome, 107; versus election, 84–85

raising your hand, x, 89, 92, 98–100
reciprocity, 44–45
recognition, 85, 90, 94; accepting, 91; as advancement, 115; advantage, xxv, 4, 82, 89–104, 91; benefits, 93; culture of, 94; definition, 92, 93, 103; dilemma, 90; getting, 92, 96, 103, 110; lack of, 102
recognition dilemma, the, 90–91, 101
reflection, 130
relationships, xix, xxiv, xxv, 3, 4, 26, 41, 101; with boss, 52–53; building, 2, 3, 5, 6, 16, 40, 47, 96; challenging, 13; chemistry, 45; feedback and, 131; maintaining, 48–49, 75; mentoring, 38–39, 43, 44, 51–52, 116; mutual benefit, 45–46; networking, 2, 6, 10, 12, 14; power, 39, 66; prioritizing, 4; reciprocity, 44–45; sponsoring, 38–39, 43, 44, 51–52, 116; variety, 46, 50
respect, 25–26, 62, 64, 66, 96, 111, 139, 151
responsibility: accepting, xxiii, 52, 69; to address discrimination, 143; empowerment and, xxviii; home life, 19, 24; for life balance, 26; for own success, xxiv; for taking credit, 95, 102; work, 37, 42, 60
results, 5, 21, 23, 51, 53, 81, 84, 126, 140, 151; and advancement, 111–120; behavior and, 79; of coaching, 169; of credibility, 61; executive presence, 100–101; of feedback, 128–129, 133, 137; focus on, 76; measurement, 87, 163, 170; of mentorship, 40, 43; misrepresenting, 95; as motivation, 4; networking, 2–3, 6, 12–16; performance, xxv, 73–74, 78, 80–81, 111; prioritization, 160; recognition or reward for, 85, 87, 94, 103; sharing (taking credit,

results (*cont.*)
   communicating), 74, 76, 80,
      82–83, 88, 91–92, 99, 102–103,
      160; of sponsorship, 43; tracking,
      77; using, 74, 97–98; of workforce
      diversity, xx, xxviii; work out-
      comes, 60
role models for women, xxii, 42, 150
role of men: executive men,
      xxvi–xxvii, 156, 162; guilt, 26,
      30; promotion of women, 41;
      stay-at-home dad, 24. *See also*
      roles
role of women, xxvi, 78; coaching,
      68, 74, 137, 141, 149; effects
      when women work, 23; executive
      women, xix, xxvii, 5, 34, 63, 75,
      122, 162; pressures for women,
      23, 34, 108; in the workplace, 24
roles: acknowledging, 99; advance-
      ment, 106, 113; coaching, xxvii,
      136; competencies, 119; expecta-
      tions, 56, 63; leadership, ix, xviii,
      xx, xxii–xxiii, 56, 58, 66, 109,
      165, 166; managing, 33; models,
      xviii, xxii, 2, 150; networking, 5;
      new, xvii, xxii, 10, 18, 36, 75, 77,
      82–83, 105, 120; passive, 107;
      perception, 56, 70; personal, 18,
      28; preference, 147; senior, xxv;
      structure, 34, 111–112; tradi-
      tional, 24; unfavorable, 99;
      validation, 97. *See also* mentor-
      ship; role of men; role of women;
      sponsorship

Sandberg, Sheryl, xvii
seat at the table, 66–67
self-awareness, 101, 131
self-image, 58
self-improvement, 127–128, 130–131,
      133
Shambaugh, Rebecca, 107, 159
Shipman, Claire, xx, 20, 108, 117

signposting, 94–95, 102
Simon, Stormy, 67, 165
sponsorship, xi, xxii, 9; accessibility,
      38; advantage, xxv, 37–54;
      benefits, 40–41, 43, 89, 90, 102,
      167; boss as, 52–53; commitment,
      43; definition, 38–39; dilemma,
      38–39; evaluating, 50; feedback
      from, 131; finding, 38–41, 46, 48;
      importance, 38, 40; lack of, 39;
      men as, xxvi–xxvii, 101, 157;
      programs, 40, 51, 166; relation-
      ships, 45, 48–50, 116; three
      conditions, 44; versus mentorship,
      38, 41–42; women as, 42. *See also*
      mentor
sponsorship dilemma, the, 38–39
stakeholders, ix, xxii, xxxiv, 82, 129
status and reputation, 59
status quo, 19
stereotype, 12, 78
Strober, Joanna, 23, 35
style, 3, 16, 50, 56–60, 64, 68, 70,
      100–101, 120; communication,
      65; leadership, xx, 57, 98, 126,
      129, 134; presentation, 96;
      versus executive presence, 66;
      work, 33
success, xxiv–xxvii, xxix–xxx, 1, 18,
      36, 38, 44–45, 48, 99, 127–128,
      140, 162, 166; credit for, 52,
      92–94; define, xxiii, 24–25, 96,
      106–108, 110–111, 123, 160, 165;
      elements of, 5–7, 51, 60, 67, 76,
      85; indicators, 76; in leadership,
      xxii, xxvi–xxvii, 53, 57; measure-
      ment, 81–82, 84

Tague, Kathryn, 1
talent management, xxviii, 116, 167
Ten Ways to Say No, 31
Tiara syndrome, the, 107
Thompson, Annette, 73
Thompson, Matt, 166–167

upward mobility, 78

validation, 38, 93
value: knowing your, 97; of mentors, 39, 43; of sponsors, 43; what others value, 94, 96; women's, xxi; your, 18, 36, 90–91, 97
values-in-action, 60
volunteering, 90, 98, 103

what women want, 109, 165
White, Nita, 19
Wilderotter, Maggie, 76

women in leadership, ix, xv, xvii; advancement, xxii–xxiii, 106, 123, 163, 167, 170; balance of, 166; benefits of, xix–xx, 162, 167, 170; benefits to, 41, 54; bias and, 148, 156; business case for, xxi, 165; challenges, xviii; development programs, 168; executive presence and, 58, 60; importance of, 160; lack of, xix, xxix, 145; new advantage, 161, 162, 170; nine advantages, xxiv–xxv; success of, xxvii
Wright, Elease, 108

About the Authors

HOWARD J. MORGAN is a cofounder and managing director at the Leadership Research Institute (LRI), as well as the cofounder of 50 Top Coaches. He has been named one of the world's top 50 coaches, recognized as 1 of 5 coaches with "a proven track record of success," and has published several books. His clients include global businesses in the financial services, manufacturing, management consulting, communication, media and high-tech industries.

Howard's understanding of the demands of executive leadership come from 17 years of experience as a line executive and executive vice president in industry and government. He specializes in executive coaching as a strategic change management tool leading to improved customer/employee satisfaction and overall corporate performance, and has done significant work coaching executives on the art of managing managers. He has worked with many executive committees of the world's largest organizations on improving corporate and executive performance.

Howard has published several books, including *The Art and Practice of Leadership Coaching* with Marshall Goldsmith and *50 Top Coaches*. In addition, he has published multiple articles, including "Leadership Is a Contact Sport," which was named among the top 10 articles in the last 15 years in *Strategy +Business* magazine, and a recent feature article in the American Management Association's *M World*. As a speaker, he has presented often at conferences for CEOs, the American Society for Training and Development, and The World Business Executive Coach Forum, which is the largest conference of its kind in the world.

Howard holds an MBA from Simon Fraser University and has completed advanced studies at the University of Michigan. He currently serves on three boards of directors located in Europe and the United States.

JOELLE K. JAY, PhD, is a principal at the LRI who specializes in leadership development for senior executives in Fortune 500 companies.

She is an award-winning executive coach, a popular keynote speaker, and a nationally recognized author on personal leadership. Her clear and sustainable approach to leadership has made her a sought-after expert whose strategies are used in corporate, entrepreneurial, and university settings to support and strengthen leaders worldwide.

As an executive coach, Joelle specializes in the advancement of executive women. Her leadership development program, Leadership Circles™, based on her previous book, has gained national recognition for helping companies such as MetLife, Microsoft, Intuit, and Adobe become best places for women to work.

Joelle has been a keynote speaker for leading corporations, professional associations, and academic institutions, including the Society for Human Resource Management (SHRM), the American Society for Training and Development, and multiple nonprofit organizations for women.

Joelle is the author of three books, dozens of articles, several white papers, and research reports in the field of leadership, and her award-winning research is featured in university courses on business management around the world. She was named one of the Top 29 Executive Coaches by the *Leadership Excellence* magazine and won acclaim for her article with Howard Morgan in *Leader to Leader*. Her book, *The Inner Edge: The 10 Practices of Personal Leadership*, has been endorsed by such luminaries as Marshall Goldsmith, Jim Kouzes, and Stephen Covey.

Joelle earned her PhD with an emphasis on learning and leadership from the University of Washington. In addition, she has a master's degree from Boston University and a bachelor's degree from the University of Nevada. She holds a Masters Coach Certification by the International Coach Federation. She has received numerous awards, including the valedictory R. Herz gold medal and the Gordon C. Lee award, for outstanding research. She has served on the faculty for both the University of Nevada and the University of Washington.

For more information, go to www.TheNewAdvantageBook.com.